TASTE of TREMÉ

Creole, Cajun and
Soul Food from
New Orleans's Famous
Neighborhood of Jazz

Todd-Michael St. Pierre

 Ulysses Press

First and foremost, to Randall!
Also, to NOLA: To my people, resilient and courageous, who paved their own road home,
fighting the red tape and those blue tarp blues . . . WHO DAT!
And for Uncle Lionel, thanks for the music! RIP.

Published by: Ulysses Press
          P.O. Box 3440
          Berkeley, CA 94703
          www.ulyssespress.com

ISBN: 978-1-61243-097-3
Library of Congress Catalog Number 2012940428

Printed in the United States by Bang Printing

10 9 8 7 6 5 4 3 2 1

Acquisitions Editor: Kelly Reed
Managing Editor: Claire Chun
Editors: Lauren Harrison, Nicky Leach
Proofreader: Elyce Berrigan-Dunlop
Design and layout: what!design @ whatweb.com
Front cover photographs: Drum © Mark Alan Gstohl; jazz statue © Sarah Rosedahl/www.srosedahl
    .com; crawfish boil © David Lee/shutterstock.com; peeling paint background © Jonas De Ro/
    cgtextures.com
Back cover photographs: New Orleans art © Diane Millsap/www.neworleans-art.net; crawfish
    beignets © judiswinksphotography; washboard musician © jimscottphotos.com
Interior photographs: see page 204
Food stylist: Anna Hartman-Kenzler for recipes on pages 33, 44, 53, 67, 78, 84, 91, 102, 119, 128,
    137, 151, 169

Distributed by Publishers Group West

IMPORTANT NOTE TO READERS: All references in this book to copyrighted or trademarked characters and other elements of HBO® and its television series TREME®, or other copyright and trademark holders, are used here for informational purposes only. This book is independently authored and published and is not affiliated or associated with HBO® and its television series TREME® in any way. HBO® does not authorize, sponsor, or endorse this book or any of the information contained herein.

Table of Contents

Introduction

"In the spring of 1988, I returned to New Orleans, and as soon as I smelled the air, I knew I was home. It was rich, almost sweet, like the scent of jasmine and roses around our old courtyard. I walked the streets, savoring that long lost perfume."
— *Anne Rice,* Interview with the Vampire

"There are a lot of places I like, but I like New Orleans better. There's a thousand different angles at any moment. At any time you could run into a ritual honoring some vaguely known queen. Bluebloods, titled persons like crazy drunks, lean weakly against the walls and drag themselves through the gutter. Even they seem to have insights you might want to listen to. No action seems inappropriate here. The city is one very long poem. Gardens full of pansies, pink petunias, opiates. Flower-bedecked shrines, white myrtles, bougainvillea and purple oleander stimulate your senses, make you feel cool and clear inside."
— *Bob Dylan,* Chronicles, Vol. 1

She has many names: NOLA (New Orleans, Louisiana), N'awlins, the Crescent City, the City That Care Forgot, and the Big Easy, to name but a few. In New Orleans, they say our crucifixes open out into liquor cabinets—like a beautiful battle between booze and holy water. Our Lady NOLA is either

Getting Around Tremé

The Tremé neighborhood borders North Rampart to North Claiborne and Orleans Avenue to St. Bernard Avenue. The greater Tremé area expands to North Broad Street. If you are visiting for the first time, the Visitor's Information Center at Basin Street Station (501 Basin Street) is a great resource. It is an old remodeled Southern Railway train station that has a gift shop and museum as well. They'll get you on the right track for your Tremé trek!

the mother superior of a convent or the madam of a "cathouse". . . and seldom anything in between. Decadent and divine—that's the dichotomy you'll find here! There is, after all, pretty much a bar on every other corner, next door to or across the street from a church. NOLA is simultaneously saintly and sinful, just like her cuisine.

My city is a city of extreme paradox. It is this paradox that gives her so much of her offbeat character and makes her unique amidst a sea of humdrum American cities. She's sunshine and shadows, rosaries and gris-gris charms, prayers and spells, a gospel song set to a striptease beat. Her fabulously flawed and perfectly imperfect nature is as inviting to me as the crooked trunks and limbs of the moss-draped live oaks on St. Charles Avenue.

The place in NOLA I love the most, though, is the culturally rich neighborhood of Tremé (truh-MAY), which in 2012 celebrated the 200th anniversary of its incorporation into the City of New Orleans. The Faubourg Tremé, the neighborhood's formal French name, is named for a Frenchman, Claude Tremé, who married into the family that acquired a plantation in the area just northwest of the French Quarter. The current Tremé was developed in the mid-1720s and populated by people of color. It is the oldest African-American neighborhood in the United States and was an important center of civil rights activity in the latter half of the 1800s. Its Congo Square is famous as the birthplace of jazz, the place where African slaves would gather to play native music and dance. Today, Tremé is home to artists, musicians, activists, and other cultural icons of the black community. Musicians from Tremé include Alphonse Picou, Kermit Ruffins, Lucien Barbarin, and "The King of Tremé," Shannon Powell. While predominantly African American, the population has been mixed

Tremé the HBO Series

Tremé's rich cultural roots provide the inspiration for the critically acclaimed and Peabody Award–winning HBO television show *Tremé*, which celebrates the food, music, and people that make this neighborhood and all of New Orleans so vibrant. The show begins three months after post-Katrina flooding devastated the city and explores the lives of several characters who have returned after the destruction. Although skeptical at first, most folks in New Orleans have embraced the show. Every week *Tremé* has aired, there have been numerous viewing gatherings at restaurants and bars throughout the metropolitan area.

You will find that throughout this book I reference characters and scenes from the series that I feel truly reflect the spirit of the Faubourg Tremé and other neighborhoods in the City That Care Forgot.

from the nineteenth century to the present. Jazz musicians of European ancestry such as Henry Ragas and Louis Prima also lived in Tremé.

In Tremé, music is always in the air and something wonderful is always simmering on the stove. Every Mardi Gras, you'll find krewes (Carnival organizations) of those feathered spectacles of tradition, Mardi Gras Indians, strutting their stuff in parades while jazz flows out of the windows of every funky little dive. It's next to impossible to find a bad meal in Tremé, one of NOLA's best-kept secrets. This is the food the locals like to eat, far from the French Quarter and the tourist traps! It's down-to-earth, honest-to-goodness cuisine, full of flavor.

I'm sure you've heard the terms Cajun and Creole used when it comes to the cuisine of South Louisiana. Who hasn't? Both styles are easily found in Tremé, and the rest of NOLA for that matter. But here's a little info that might be helpful in order for one to better appreciate their very distinct personalities.

Cajuns descended from Acadian (French Canadian) settlers. The French had established a colony known as Acadia in Eastern Canada. The area now includes New Brunswick, Nova Scotia, and Prince Edward Island, but in 1755, the Acadians were forced out when the land was ceded to the English and the people of the colony refused to swear allegiance to the British crown and forsake their Catholic faith. Once deported, the Acadians headed to the swamps and bayous of south Louisiana, where they established colonies around the marshes there, a twenty-two parish area known today as Acadiana. Cajun cuisine evolved in these rural parishes and throughout the Atchafalaya swamp region, where such products as rice, crawfish, and wild game were in abundance.

New Orleans's Wards

New Orleans neighborhoods are known to locals as "wards." According to Richard Campanella, author of *Bienville's Dilemma: A Historical Geography of New Orleans*, the ward system was first instituted in 1805 to delineate "voting districts, demographic units for censuses, and other municipal purposes," and underwent several revisions. Writes Campanella, "New Orleans natives with deep local roots often use the ward system in perceiving urban space. . . . Because nativity rates are much higher among black residents than whites, wards are particularly common as a spatial reference in the African-American community. Elderly natives of any race are often unfamiliar with the trendy revived faubourg names, just as many recently arrived transplants and college students are at a loss when asked what ward they live in."

Creoles, on the other hand, descended from European (mostly French and Spanish) settlers of the state who established their neighborhoods (faubourgs) in cities like New Orleans. Often the food style varied from one neighborhood to the next, depending on the country of origin of the majority of the residents. Creole cuisine evolved, in large part, out of those old world tastes and techniques, heavily influenced by the rich traditions of French cooking. Many Creole-style dishes include lots of tomatoes and/or feature a hearty bisque, and often contain the regionally plentiful shellfish like oysters, shrimp, and crab.

While New Orleans–style food is never overcooked, some dishes do need to be cooked a long time to give the flavors a chance to meld and mingle. That's the secret of achieving the trademark "jazz" of NOLA cuisine that allows it to dance down the street happily—just like at a New Orleans wedding or funeral in the Tremé!

No absence of passion. That pretty much describes the south Louisiana I know. It's not only our obvious passions for wonderful cuisine, rich musical traditions, colorful culture, or even the undeniable legacy of Louisiana sports teams like the New Orleans Saints. It is also our deeply felt passion for love and laughter, friends and family, and even for strangers, with whom we share our legendary joie de vivre. It's the passionate character of our citizens, who overcome adversity and manage to rebound stronger and prouder than before. It's a passion for holidays, festivals, and get-togethers—a passion born, in part, from knowing all too well that we'd better cherish the good times with all five senses, like a picture-perfect day, because who knows when dark clouds might return? We relish everyday happiness. We celebrate life. And we simply refuse to take any moment for granted.

The New Orleans spirit is one of survival. Even after enduring a huge event like Hurricane Katrina and more recently, the Deepwater Horizon oil spill, the people of New Orleans have bounced back stronger—and one might say even better—than before! New Orleans traditions march on, through hell and high water. And the Tremé goes on, too—thriving, proud, and full of love, life, and spectacle.

Merci beaucoup, y'all!

—Todd-Michael

Things You'll Need

---◆–◆–◆---

"It is hard to sit in silence, to watch one's youth wash away. Everything that I have professionally, and so much of what I have personally, is because of this great, fair city ... to see it being drowned like this is almost unbearable."

HARRY CONNICK JR., AFTER HURRICANE KATRINA

---◆–◆–◆---

There are some basic ingredients that are used in many recipes in this book, delicious flavors that will jazz up your pantry. One important thing to know is that while many people think of Creole- and Cajun-style food as being very hot, spicy, and blackened, it's not necessarily so. New Orleans cuisine is much more concerned with achieving the perfect seasonings and spice combination in each dish. "Spice" doesn't always equate to "hot"; down here, it usually refers to "flavor!" Simply disguising a dish with heat is unacceptable to me, and to most New Orleanians. In fact, true Big Easy cuisine focuses on combining fresh, quality ingredients to create complementary and harmonious results—memorable and flavorful dishes without the need for pepper overkill. Yes, I know some folks like their food extremely spicy. Well, that's their prerogative, but the heart of Creole and Cajun food is about achieving something more sophisticated.

 # Spice

"There is no sincerer love than the love of food."

—*GEORGE BERNARD SHAW*

The spice mixtures that follow are dry ingredients that you can use anywhere in this book where the recipe calls for Creole/Cajun spice. The terms "spice" and "seasoning" are often used interchangeably. However, any NOLA chef, either professional or amateur, will tell you that "spice" refers to the dry stuff while "seasoning" refers to the seasoned meats and vegetables used in a recipe.

There are many spice mixtures that claim to be Creole or Cajun spices. I have used most of them, and they are not bad. However, be aware that these store-bought brands usually have a lot of salt and are often overloaded with cayenne. You can't control how spicy they are, and they may include some very strange-sounding ingredients, many of which seem more like chemicals you'd expect to find in a Tulane chemistry lab than flavors you'd want to add to your food. It's not hard to make your own spice mixtures, if you have the ingredients in your spice rack. You can also experiment with ratios according to your own personal taste.

The spices used in New Orleans cooking are not always as hot as people seem to think. In fact, many NOLA cooks only use modest amounts of "hot" pepper in their dishes. That's why there are so many Louisiana hot sauces on the market. Traditionally, if you like it real hot, then you just add a few dashes of your favorite hot sauce to "spice" things up.

✦ Suck da Heads and Pinch da Tails Creole Spice

This mixture can be used to season just about anything in this book where the recipe calls for Creole/Cajun spice.

2 tablespoons onion powder
2 tablespoons garlic powder
2 tablespoons dried oregano
2 tablespoons dried basil
1 tablespoon dried thyme

1 tablespoon black pepper
1 tablespoon white pepper
1 tablespoon cayenne pepper
5 tablespoons smoked paprika
3 tablespoons salt

Combine all the ingredients in an airtight container and store in a cool, dry place for an extended shelf life of up to 1 year.

Suck Da Heads and Pinch Da Tails

The title of this homemade Creole-style dry spice mix comes from a popular phrase in south Louisiana that refers to the manner in which we peel boiled crawfish: "Pinch the tail" to loosen the meat before peeling, and "suck the head" because many people say that's where the best flavor is. Crawfish boils are popular outdoor gatherings especially during crawfish season, but thanks to crawfish farming it isn't unusual for these festive events to occur almost anytime during the warm months, and sometimes a warm month can even be November, December, or (late) February, though seldom January!

☩ All That Jazz Creole and Cajun Blast

This spice blend has all the flavors of traditional Creole or Cajun spices but with less salt than commercial brands. In fact, you can leave the salt out completely or substitute a salt alternative if you're watching your blood pressure. This mixture can be used to season just about anything in this book where the recipe calls for Creole/Cajun spice.

Makes about 1½ cups

½ cup garlic powder
½ cup onion powder
4 tablespoons smoked paprika
2 tablespoons cayenne pepper
2 tablespoons black pepper

3 teaspoons celery seeds
3 teaspoons chili powder
2 teaspoons salt
2 teaspoons lemon pepper
1 teaspoon ground nutmeg

Combine all the ingredients in an airtight container and store in a cool, dry place for an extended shelf life of up to 1 year.

☩ In the Mix Gumbo Spice

Gumbo filé (FEE-lay) is an herb made from ground sassafras leaves. It can be found in most large chain grocery stores in the United States. Filé powder can be added before or after a gumbo is cooked and is often used when okra is not available. This adds an earthy flavor to the dish and also will thicken it up a bit if you find your gumbo too souplike. The word filé roughly translates to "string," a reference to its thickening properties.

Makes about 1 cup

4 tablespoons filé powder
2 tablespoons chopped fresh thyme
2 tablespoons chili powder
2 tablespoons smoked paprika

2 tablespoons white pepper
4 tablespoons black pepper
2 tablespoons cayenne pepper

Combine all the ingredients in a small bowl and store in a tightly sealed jar for an extended shelf life of up to 1 year.

⇸ Seasoning

> "New Orleans food is as delicious as the less criminal forms of sin."
>
> —*MARK TWAIN*

Seasoning refers to the ingredients that are not dry in your recipe. So when I say "seasoning" you should expect to be chopping vegetables or cutting up some meat because, in Louisiana cooking, "seasonings" refers to the vegetables and meats used to flavor a dish.

Vegetable seasonings usually consist of onion, celery, and bell peppers, with some adding garlic as well. Many grocery stores in Louisiana have Creole seasonings in the fresh vegetable section, already chopped and ready to go. I've even seen them in the frozen food section. Finding seasoning meats like tasso, andouille, or pickled pork outside the South, and even beyond the borders of Louisiana, may be a challenge. I've included these meats here and either given you a recipe or told you where you can order and have them shipped to your door.

Andouille Sausage

Several recipes throughout this book call for andouille (aun-dooie) sausage, made from a coarsely ground smoked meat made using pork, pepper, onions, and seasonings. Brought to Louisiana by German or French immigrants, it's almost hamlike, unlike most sausages, in which the meat is ground finer.

As Louisiana cuisine has become more popular, many non-natives have tried to make this delicious sausage. Most are just a ground pork sausage with a little cayenne added for that "Cajun" taste. Don't be fooled by the sausage you might see in your grocer's meat case. I have tried these and although most are pretty good, they aren't like the real deal. However, there are some brands of andouille that are not made in Louisiana that come close, such as Aidells Cajun Style Andouille.

Cajun Grocer (www.cajungrocer.com) is my favorite place to order anything you need to cook original NOLA cuisine. There are a lot of andouille brands here, so research what others suggest as being the best. I've used most all of them, and they are all better than the non-native brands. My favorites are Poche's and Big Easy. Give them a try after you've tasted the real thing.

✦ The Holy Trinity (Wit or Wit-out da Pope)

The Cajun and Creole seasoning known as the Holy Trinity is the foundation for many south Louisiana dishes, including red beans and rice, gumbo, jambalaya, and étouffée. Consisting of finely chopped onion, celery, and bell pepper, its origins are the mirepoix techniques established in eighteenth-century French cuisine. Mirepoix is used in cooking techniques around the world, and variations use garlic, parsley, or shallots, but the Holy Trinity is unique to Louisiana. Finely chopped garlic is the optional fourth ingredient, called "The Pope." The Holy Trinity is best when it's freshly chopped, but you can freeze it in an airtight zip-top bag or container for up to 3 months.

Makes 3 to 4 cups

1 medium white onion
4 ribs celery
1 large green bell pepper
4 garlic cloves (optional)

Combine the onion, celery, bell pepper, and garlic, if using, in a food processor and pulse until finely chopped. You can also do this by hand using your favorite knife. Run the mixture through a fine-mesh sieve to strain the excess juice.

Tremé Brass Band

Uncle Lionel Batiste, who passed away in 2012, was a bass drummer and vocalist, as well as an assistant leader for the Tremé Brass Band. He was also known for being a skilled kazoo player. Lionel has been a mentor for many young musicians, including Kermit Ruffins. The Tremé Brass Band has been the launching pad for several respected New Orleans jazz musicians, including James Andrews (trumpet), Elliot Callier and Frederick Sheppard (sax), Corey Henry (trombone), and Kirk Joseph (sousophone). In 2006, the band was recognized with the National Heritage Fellowship award by the National Endowment of the Arts.

→ Cajun Tasso

Many call tasso (TAH-so) "Cajun ham," but it is unique in its own right and isn't eaten like ham. Made from lean strips of boneless pork that are marinated in a special seasoning and then heavily smoked, this Cajun delicacy is primarily used in south Louisiana cooking as a seasoning. Tasso is sliced or diced into small pieces and added to other dishes to add authentic south Louisiana spice-of-life flavor. Leftover tasso freezes well in a zip-top bag for up to 6 months.

Makes about 16 (8-ounce) servings

1 gallon (16 cups) water
1 cup pickling salt
½ cup sugar
⅓ cup Prague powder #1 (pink
   curing salt)
7 to 8 pounds boneless pork
   shoulder roast
2 to 4 tablespoons cayenne pepper,
   as needed

3 tablespoons kosher salt
2 tablespoons black pepper
2 tablespoons white pepper
1½ tablespoons smoked paprika
1½ tablespoons ground cinnamon
1½ tablespoons garlic powder

Combine the water, pickling salt, sugar, and Prague powder in a very large glass or plastic bowl (not metal). Refrigerate until the liquid is around 40°F. Add the pork roast to the brining liquid and be sure it's completely covered with the brining liquid. Cover and refrigerate for 1 to 3 days. The longer the better, giving the meat time to soak up the flavorings. Don't let the temperature drop below 38°F during the brining process.

Remove the roast from the brine and rinse thoroughly, then place the roast on a wire rack and let it dry completely. You might want to put the roast in front of a small fan for 1 to 2 hours.

In a small bowl, combine the cayenne pepper, kosher salt, black pepper, white pepper, paprika, cinnamon, and garlic powder. Rub the mixture onto the roast. Make sure you cover the roast completely, and don't be shy. There should be at least ⅛ inch of spice on the roast.

Prepare a smoker or grill, and heat to 150 to 160°F. You will want to hot-smoke this over indirect heat, or at least 2 feet from the coals. I don't recommend a water pan for this; the idea is to completely dry the meat out. Smoke the roast at 150 to 160°F for 2 hours, then increase the cooking temperature to 170 to 180°F and smoke until the internal temperature of the meat is 150°F, about 2 hours.

Place the roast on the wire rack to cool in front of a fan again for about 1 hour. Cut the roast into 8-ounce portions and package in individual vacuum-sealed bags. Refrigerate for up to 4 days or freeze for up to 1 year.

✦ Pickled Pork

Pickled meats have their roots in the days before refrigeration when meats were preserved by being brined (or pickled) in large barrels. When a hog was slaughtered, the meat was immediately pickled to prevent spoilage. Pickled pork is still used in Creole and Cajun cooking and is readily found in grocery stores in the region. If you want to purchase pickled pork, you probably won't be able to find it outside of the South, but you can order it online from Cajun Grocer (www.cajungrocer.com). Don't confuse pickled pork with salt pork, which is more closely related to bacon. You can also easily make your own using the standard recipe here. Pickled pork makes a wonderful addition to pots of beans and gumbos and can be added to any dish that calls for bacon or salt pork without adding extra salt.

Makes 2 pounds

1 quart (4 cups) white vinegar
½ cup mustard seeds
5 whole cloves
5 allspice berries
½ teaspoon coarsely ground red pepper
6 bay leaves
6 garlic cloves

½ medium white onion, coarsely chopped
1 tablespoon kosher salt
1 tablespoon black peppercorns
1 pinch Prague powder #1 (pink curing salt)
2 pounds boneless pork roast (cheaper cuts are fine)

In a 2-quart saucepan, combine the vinegar, mustard seeds, cloves, allspice, red pepper, bay leaves, garlic, onion, salt, black peppercorns, and Prague powder, and bring to a boil over high heat. Let boil for 5 minutes, then remove from the heat. Let cool to room temperature, and then refrigerate until cold.

When the pickling mixture is completely cold, add the pork, making sure it is completely covered with the liquid. Stir to remove any air bubbles. Cover and refrigerate for 3 to 4 days. This must be cooked before eating. Any portions that are not used after 4 days may be frozen in a vacuum-sealed bag for up to 6 months.

✒ And First You Make a Roux . . .

"Cooking is like sex: You do the best you can with what you have."

—*JAMES BARBER*

Using a roux to make sauces and thicken liquids is a classic technique in French cooking and a common practice in cooking New Orleans dishes, which are heavily influenced by NOLA's French past. So in order to make everything from gumbos to étouffées you will first need to make a roux. This is an art form in itself. You may have to practice and burn a few before you get the hang of it. Even my Maw-Maw, who was the best at making a roux as I ever saw, would burn her roux every now and then. It takes time and constant attention to make a fantastic roux. Fortunately, flour and oil are cheap. For those who just cannot do a roux, you have the option to buy it already prepared and in a jar. These do the trick and make your cooking time much shorter. Go to www.cajungrocer .com and search for "roux."

Dry Roux

A great way to make gumbo lighter in calories is to use a dry roux. Made without oil, a dry roux is a blessing to gumbo lovers watching their fat intake. It's easy to make, stores well refrigerated in an airtight container, and makes an authentic Louisiana gumbo.

You may find various brands of roux mixes in the grocery store, which include directions for how to use them, but other ingredients are often added for seasoning and to extend their shelf lives that sound like they belong in chemistry lab and not your stomach. These products are also much more expensive than just making the roux yourself.

There are two methods for making a dry roux: a skillet is used for smaller quantities, while larger quantities are baked in the oven (see page 20 for recipes). Store in a glass jar or plastic container in a cool, dry place for as long as you want. Just like storing raw flour, the only enemies here are moisture and hungry bugs.

↝ Traditional Roux

A roux sounds easy, but you must have patience and stamina to make a good one. Don't rush it, and make sure you don't burn it. Take it slow and easy, just like they do in the Tremé. A good traditional dark roux can take you 30-plus minutes to make.

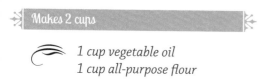

Makes 2 cups

1 cup vegetable oil
1 cup all-purpose flour

Heat a heavy 10 to 12-inch skillet over medium-low heat. Add the oil and allow it to heat. Slowly add the flour while constantly stirring. Continue to cook, stirring constantly, until the desired color is reached. The longer you cook the roux, the darker it will get. A dark roux will add a smoky flavor to the dish you are preparing. Take care not to burn it.

↝ Skillet Roux

This dry roux should be cooked fresh for each recipe. Extra roux can be stored in the refrigerator, but must be used quickly, as it becomes rancid very fast.

Makes 1 to 2 cups

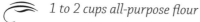

1 to 2 cups all-purpose flour

Place the flour in a large, heavy pot or a deep cast-iron skillet and toast over medium heat, stirring constantly until the flour is close to the color of peanut butter or pecans, 15 to 20 minutes. It will be a lighter color than a traditional roux made with oil. The lighter color will result in a dark gumbo.

↝ Oven-Baked Roux

This dry roux should be cooked fresh for each recipe. Extra roux can be stored in the refrigerator, but must be used quickly, as it becomes rancid very fast.

Makes 3 to 4 cups

3 to 4 cups all-purpose flour

Preheat the oven to 400°F. Place the flour in a heavy 10 to 12-inch cast-iron skillet or Dutch oven, and bake, stirring every 10 minutes, until it reaches an evenly browned peanut butter color, 45 to 60 minutes total. Depending on your oven, the cooking time may vary.

St. Louis Cemetery and African-American History

To gain a better understanding of the history of African Americans in the Tremé, take a tour of the St. Louis Cemetery #1, which was founded as a place of interment in 1796. St. Louis Cemetery is the oldest of all the cemeteries in New Orleans. This picturesque cemetery is home to the tomb of Voodoo Queen Marie Laveau, said to be the most visited gravesite in the state of Louisiana, and other famous citizens. All burials are above-ground in tombs in New Orleans, to keep graves from being flooded out.

St. Louis Cemetery has three locations throughout the city, with St. Louis #1 and #2 being the oldest and most famous. Many prominent black residents, politicians, and entertainers of New Orleans and the Faubourg Tremé claim St. Louis Cemetery as their final resting place. The most notable graves here are Homer Plessy of the famous Plessy v. Ferguson Supreme Court decision; Ernest N. "Dutch" Morial, first African-American mayor of the city; and, as noted above, Marie Laveau, believed to be interred in the Glapion family crypt. They are all in cemetery #1. If you visit cemetery #2, three blocks behind #1, you'll find musicians Danny Barker and Ernie K. Doe, as well as several Jean Lafitte pirates. Tomb styles include parapet, pedestal, pediment, society, and wall vaults, and the style of tomb often indicates the standing of the person occupying it. It's quite

fascinating to walk around the cemetery and see the different architectural styles of these final resting places. To see some very elaborate tombs, visit cemetery #3, about 2 miles from the French Quarter on Esplanade Avenue. Take one of the hundreds of walking tours available. They will be able to tell you so much more than I can here.

Breaking the Fast

"I was seven before I realized you could eat breakfast
with your pants on."

CHRISTOPHER MOORE

Breakfast in New Orleans usually consists of coffee and a pastry. Coffeehouses go way back in New Orleans, long before the chain shops that you see on every corner in this day and age. Coffee is also a staple for most any meal other than breakfast. And what is coffee without a sweet pastry to accompany it? This has been a NOLA tradition for maybe a century or so.

The tradition of having a late breakfast, or brunch, sometime between 10:30 a.m. and lunchtime is a natural one in New Orleans. After a late night of celebration and partying, especially on Saturday and Sunday, it's just normal to sleep a bit late and then go have a substantial brunch to cure your hangover.

From Café du Monde and Mother's to Brennan's and the Court of Two Sisters's famous brunch to Tremé's own Dizzy's Café, breakfast in New Orleans comes as easily to the residents as a second line parade and jazz funerals.

Café

New Orleans coffee (aka "Cafe Noir") has a distinctive chocolate-caramel flavor, intensely dark color, thick consistency, and lower-than-usual caffeine content, thanks to its secret ingredient: chicory. Chicory is a coffeelike substance made from the dried, roasted roots of a bitter perennial herb. According to New Orleans locals, it's what makes New Orleans coffee worth writing home about. Louisiana's love of strong coffee is described best in this traditional Cajun French rhyme:

Noir comme le Diable; Fort comme la Mort;
Doux comme l'Amour;
Et chaud comme l'Enfer.

English Translation:
Black as the Devil;
Strong as Death;
Sweet as Love;
And hot as Hell.

A World Coffee Destination

Coffee first came to North America by way of New Orleans back in the mid-1700s; in fact, Latin American coffee beans have long been imported into North America through the mouth of the Mississippi River. This availability of raw beans provided a catalyst for an industry for roasting and distributing coffee throughout the United States and Canada. Today, one-third of all coffee imported to North America lands first in the Port of New Orleans, as is evidenced by the dozen or so coffee roasting companies, from the local New Orleans Famous French Market Coffee to Community Coffee to the world's largest roasting plant in the world, which produces Folgers Coffee.

Free women of color, many of whom probably resided in the Tremé in the early nineteenth century, set up coffee stands on the streets where they served their own unique blends of coffee. One of these women, Rose Nicaud, became the very first coffee vendor in the Big Easy. Rose was a slave who bought her freedom with what she earned at her coffee stand near St. Louis Cathedral. These street vendors later went on to establish independently owned coffee shops throughout the city. Presently, one of my favorite coffee shops in all of New Orleans is Faubourg Marigny's Cafe Rose Nicaud (632 Frenchman Street), named in her honor.

✈ Brew HA! HA! Café au Lait

New Orleans–style café au lait has its origins in the classic French method of mixing strong, dark blends with equal parts cream or milk, and has become the Crescent City coffee drink of choice. What sets many New Orleans roasted coffees apart is the use of the chicory root as a flavor enhancer, and many locals say it's essential to the true NOLA café experience. Community New Orleans Blend, Café Du Monde, and French Market brands are all excellent choices. It is best consumed while enjoying the famous New Orleans doughnuts known as beignets (ben-YAYS).

 Serves 6 to 12

3 cups whole milk
½ cup heavy cream
3 cups hot Louisiana coffee with
chicory

Combine the milk and cream in a medium saucepan and bring just to a boil over medium heat (bubbles will form around the edge of the pan). Remove from the heat. Fill each cup halfway with coffee, and then pour in the hot milk mixture to fill the cup.

Café Du Monde Coffee

In the HBO *Tremé* television series, after the John Goodman character, Creighton Bernette, decides to take the big drink in the Mississippi, one of the last things he does is stop by Café Du Monde and stand in one of the long lines to order beignets (doubtless, he had himself a cup of café au lait, too, because what's a beignet without an au lait?). I guess that was something he decided he had to have one more time before passing on to that parade float in the sky.

World-famous Café Du Monde in the New Orleans French Market may well be the oldest coffeehouse in America! You can order authentic Café Du Monde and other New Orleans coffees, the same kinds that are served in Tremé and the French Quarter, online or at many grocers like World Market, and most national chains carry at least one variety of Louisiana-roasted coffee.

✈ The Blississippi (Frosty Mochas)

A frozen concoction will cool you off on those hot, humid summer days in the Tremé. This one will make your friends and family smile and dream about those warm days in subtropical New Orleans.

Serves 3 to 4

1 cup hot coffee
6 tablespoons chocolate syrup
1 pint vanilla ice cream, softened
1 cup cold coffee

Combine the hot coffee and chocolate syrup in a blender, and blend until smooth. Allow to cool to room temperature, then add the ice cream and the cold coffee. Blend until smooth. Pour into tall glasses and serve immediately.

✦ Pastry

Lead me not into temptation; I can find the way myself.

— *RITA MAE BROWN*

Tiana: Beignets? Got me a fresh batch just waitin' for you.
Big Daddy: Well, keep 'em comin' 'til I pass out!

—*DISNEY'S THE PRINCESS AND THE FROG*

We all know that the French are famous for their irresistible pastries. It is a natural phenomenon that New Orleans, with its strong French influence, also has some of the best doughy treats in the world. But the region's Spanish and Italian influences have also contributed greatly to the grand breakfast pastries found in the Crescent City.

Many folks find baking an arduous undertaking. The following recipes are not that difficult to make. Give them a try. You will not be disappointed, and your sweet tooth will appreciate your labors!

The Official Doughnut!

This is the official state doughnut of Louisiana. It has Spanish and Islamic roots, and many say that this famous tradition was brought to the city by Ursuline Nuns of France in the early eighteenth century. This fried treat is very similar to a variety of pastries where yeast dough is deep-fried and then covered with a topping. Confectioners' sugar is the traditional New Orleans topping. You can get premade beignet mixes at a grocer, or order online.

→ Totally Traditional Beignets

It's worth repeating: You must have a cup of café au lait to go with your beignets (ben-YAYS), preferably at the Café Du Monde, the beignet and café au lait mecca of the world. Café du Monde sells their brand of beignet mix that is about as close as you can get to the real thing, and you can also find their coffee if you look hard enough. You just won't have the ambience of actually being there.

Makes 8

1 packet (2¼ teaspoons) active dry
  yeast
1½ cups warm water (110°F)
½ cup granulated sugar
1 teaspoon salt
2 large eggs

1 cup evaporated milk
7 cups all-purpose flour, divided
¼ cup shortening
1 quart (4 cups) vegetable oil, for
  frying
1 cup confectioners' sugar

In a large bowl, dissolve the yeast in the warm water and let stand for 5 minutes. Add the sugar, salt, eggs, and evaporated milk, and whisk to combine. Add 4 cups of the flour and whisk until you have a smooth batter. Add the shortening, then the remaining 3 cups of flour, and mix until you have a thick dough. Cover with a towel and refrigerate for 24 hours.

In a large, heavy pot, heat the vegetable oil to 360°F, and line a rimmed baking sheet with paper towels. On a floured surface, roll out the dough to ⅛ inch thick, and cut into 2½-inch squares. When the oil is hot, add the beignets. Do not add too many at one time; they need room to fry evenly. If the beignets do not pop up to the surface almost immediately, the oil is not hot enough. Turn once during frying until both sides are golden brown. Drain on the paper towels. Shake confectioners' sugar over the hot beignets and serve warm.

→ Marais Street Pear and Pecan Muffins

Pecans and pears are native to the South and will grow just about anywhere where the climate is warm for the majority of the year. So it's not uncommon to see pecans and pear preserves as a staple in a Tremé pantry. This recipe uses both for a tasty muffin that will satisfy any sweet tooth in the morning.

Makes 12

1½ cups all-purpose flour
½ cup plus 3 to 4 tablespoons
   packed brown sugar, divided
2¼ teaspoons baking powder
1 teaspoon ground cinnamon
½ teaspoon ground ginger
½ teaspoon salt
1 medium pear, peeled and finely
   chopped

1 large egg
½ cup plain yogurt
1 teaspoon vanilla extract
½ cup vegetable oil
3 to 4 tablespoons finely chopped
   pecans

Preheat the oven to 350°F, and butter 12 standard muffin cups. Sift the flour, ½ cup of the brown sugar, baking powder, cinnamon, ginger, and salt into a large bowl, rubbing the sugar through the sifter. Stir in the chopped pear. In a medium bowl, whisk together the egg, yogurt, vanilla, and oil. Add the wet ingredients to the dry ingredients, and stir until just combined; do not over mix.

Fill the prepared muffin cups about two-thirds full with batter. In a small bowl, mix the pecans and remaining brown sugar, and sprinkle the topping over each muffin. Bake until lightly browned and a cake tester or toothpick inserted in the center comes out clean, 20 to 25 minutes. Cool for 30 minutes on a wire rack and serve. Store in a cool, dry place for a couple of days and then refrigerate. These warm up nicely in the microwave.

↝ North Derbigny Street Lost Bread (Born Again)

Pain perdu ("lost bread" in French) is the delicious New Orleans version of what is commonly called French toast. Pain perdu was invented in New Orleans as a way of using up stale French bread by immersing it in an egg mixture and pan-frying it in butter. In France, this is normally a dessert; in New Orleans, it is most often served for breakfast.

Serves 6

1 cup brown sugar
1 tablespoon light corn syrup
6 tablespoons unsalted butter
⅓ cup heavy whipping cream
1 teaspoon vanilla extract, divided
¾ cup pecans, chopped

½ cup whole milk
3 large eggs
pinch of salt
½ teaspoon ground cinnamon
6 to 7 slices French bread, about ¾ inch thick

The night before serving, butter a 9 x 13-inch pan. In a medium saucepan over low heat, combine the brown sugar, corn syrup, butter, and cream. Stir constantly until the butter is melted and the ingredients are smooth. Remove from the heat and stir in ½ teaspoon of the vanilla. Pour the warm caramel mixture into the prepared pan and spread evenly. Sprinkle the pecans over the top.

In a large bowl, whisk together the milk, eggs, salt, the remaining ½ teaspoon vanilla, and the cinnamon. One slice at a time, immerse the bread in the egg mixture, making sure each slice thoroughly soaks up the egg mixture. Lay the bread in the pan, over the caramel and pecan mixture. Repeat with the remaining slices. Cover and refrigerate overnight.

The next morning, preheat your oven to 425°F. Uncover the pan and bake until the bottom is bubbling and the toast is golden brown, about 20 minutes. Let stand for a couple of minutes, then invert onto a platter and serve.

→ My Noisy Neighbor's Strawberry Muffins

In season 1 of the HBO series, perhaps Davis McAlary should have given his neighbor one of these treats before his party, and then Allan might not have called the police because of all the noise. You might assume they had the stereo blasting, but McAlary tells his guests that in New Orleans there are no stereos at parties—the music is often live and improvised. So true! Also true is that some of the sweetest strawberries in the world are grown on the north shore of Lake Pontchartrain, and these muffins were originally made with fresh, ripe Louisiana strawberries grown in Ponchatoula, Louisiana. I would put these up against any berries grown anywhere in the world. Use fresh berries for this recipe, if possible; check out the ones at your local farmer's market.

Makes 12

½ cup unsalted butter, at room
  temperature
1½ cups granulated sugar, plus
  more for topping
4 large eggs
1 teaspoon vanilla extract
3 cups all-purpose flour

1 teaspoon baking powder
½ teaspoon baking soda
½ teaspoon salt
½ teaspoon finely grated lemon zest
1 cup buttermilk
1 cup fresh or frozen sliced
  strawberries

Preheat the oven to 350°F, and butter 12 standard muffin cups or line with paper liners. In a large bowl with an electric handheld mixer on high speed, cream the butter and sugar; beat in the eggs one at a time, beating after each addition. Blend in the vanilla.

In a second large bowl, stir together the flour, baking powder, baking soda, and salt. With a wooden spoon, stir the flour mixture into the egg mixture. Gradually stir in the lemon zest and buttermilk until the dry ingredients are just moistened; do not overmix.

Spoon the batter into the prepared muffin cups, filling each cup about two-thirds full. Evenly spoon sliced strawberries onto the center of each muffin, and sprinkle each with a little granulated sugar. Bake until the tops of the muffins spring back when pressed, about 20 minutes. Cool in the pan on a wire rack for 5 minutes, then gently turn the muffins directly onto the rack. Serve warm.

✦ Cousin's Husband's Uncle's Fig Bread

The fig tree is common in all of Louisiana, and you can find figs in many a backyard in New Orleans. One common method of preserving this fast-ripening fruit, which has a very short shelf life in New Orleans, is to make fig bread. This delicious sweet bread freezes well wrapped in plastic wrap and will provide a wonderful treat until the next crop of fruit bears next year.

Makes 2 loaves

3 large eggs
2½ cups sugar
2 cups ripe mashed figs
¾ cup vegetable oil
3 cups all-purpose flour
2 teaspoons baking soda

1 teaspoon salt
½ teaspoon ground cinnamon
½ cup buttermilk
1¼ cup chopped pecans
¼ cup of Southern Comfort
 (optional)

Preheat the oven to 350°F. Butter 2 (5 x 9-inch) loaf pans, and dust the bottom and sides with flour.

In a large bowl with a handheld mixer on low speed, beat the eggs. Add the sugar and beat well on medium speed. Stir in the mashed figs and oil. In a second large bowl, sift together the flour, baking soda, salt, and cinnamon. Add the fig mixture and the buttermilk to the flour mixture, and mix on medium to medium-high speed to beat well. Fold in the pecans and Southern Comfort, if using. Bake until the internal temperature is 200°F, about 1 hour. To test this, turn the bread out of the loaf pan and insert a meat thermometer in the bottom of the loaf. You can also use the thump test by tapping on the bottom and if it sounds hollow, it is done.

Eggs

He that but looketh on a plate of ham and eggs to lust after it hath already committed breakfast in his heart.

— *C. S. LEWIS*

To be honest, no one does eggs like they do in the Tremé and French Quarter. From eggs Benedict and eggs Sardou to the most creative omelets around, nowhere else but in New Orleans will you find recipes like those I've included here. Exquisite examples of the brunch fare you might find on a Saturday or Sunday morning at Brennan's, the Court of Two Sisters, and Tremé's own Lil' Dizzy's Café on Esplanade Avenue follow.

A Tremé Morning Stroll

Café Tremé, located at 1501 St. Phillip Street at North Villere, is the perfect place for a quick breakfast and a cup of the (dark and distinctive) local java! After breakfast, head over to Louis Armstrong Park, home to Congo Square. If you're there at the right time, you might find a local street musician performing jazz or blues either solo or with a group. If you're lucky, you might catch the Tremé Brass Band leading a jazz funeral or a second line parade somewhere around the St. Louis Cemetery. Louis Armstrong Park is home to concerts from famous and up-and-coming musicians. During Jazz Fest you can attend the Congo Square Rhythms Festival, which celebrates the percussive influences of African, Caribbean, and Latin American music on the city and the development of jazz. Here you'll also find Perseverance Hall, the oldest Masonic Lodge in the state of Louisiana. Other highlights are the bronze statues of legendary musicians Louis Armstrong and Sidney Bechet, which can be seen near North Rampart Street, between St. Ann and Dumaine streets.

Sidney Bechet

→ Quinn's Quaint Crab Quiche

This take on the pielike dish that "real men don't eat" will make any of the male species come back for seconds and even fourths. It must be the crab or something. You can usually find par-baked pie shells in the frozen-food aisle of your local grocer. If not, line the pie shell with foil and fill with a layer of dried beans. Bake at 350°F until the shell is a light golden color. You want it cooked just enough so that the egg mixture won't make it soggy. Be careful not to completely cook the pie crust.

Serves 4

1 tablespoon unsalted butter
2 tablespoons minced shallots
1 cup fresh white or lump crabmeat
(fresh preferred but packaged
will do)
1 tablespoon all-purpose flour
1½ cups shredded Swiss cheese,
divided

1 (9-inch) pie shell, par-baked
3 large eggs
1 cup half-and-half
½ teaspoon salt
dash Louisiana-style hot sauce or
white pepper
dash ground nutmeg
½ cup minced parsley

Preheat the oven to 350°F.

Melt the butter in a medium skillet over medium heat, and sauté the shallots until tender, about 2 minutes. Stir in the crabmeat and flour. Sprinkle ¾ cup of the cheese in the bottom of the pie shell, then spread the crab mixture on top. Sprinkle on the remaining ¾ cup of cheese. In a medium bowl, whisk together the eggs, half-and-half, salt, hot sauce or white pepper, nutmeg, and parsley until combined. Pour the egg mixture into shell over the cheese and crab mixture. Bake until puffy and golden brown, 25 to 30 minutes.

Irma's Eggs Sardou

Eggs Sardou—poached eggs enrobed in hollandaise sauce and served on an artichoke on a bed of creamed spinach—was created at world-famous Antoine's Restaurant in the French Quarter. Antoine Alciatore created and named this dish for nineteenth-century French playwright Victorien Sardou, who was visiting the city. This rich and delicious version is named after the Soul Queen of New Orleans, Irma Thomas, one of my all-time favorites.

Serves 2

 CREAMED SPINACH
1 pint (2 cups) heavy cream
1 cup cooked, chopped fresh spinach
pinch freshly grated nutmeg
pinch cayenne pepper
2 teaspoons Louisiana-style hot
  sauce
5 drops Worcestershire sauce
1 teaspoon sea salt

 HOLLANDAISE SAUCE
2 teaspoons apple cider vinegar
2 teaspoons freshly squeezed lemon
  juice
3 egg yolks
½ cup warm clarified unsalted
  butter
1 dash Louisiana-style hot sauce
few drops Worcestershire sauce
sea salt and cayenne pepper

 POACHED EGGS
1 teaspoon white vinegar
4 large eggs

ASSEMBLY
4 artichoke bottoms (canned is fine)
paprika, for sprinkling

FOR THE CREAMED SPINACH: In a medium saucepan over medium-low heat, bring the cream to a simmer and reduce to about 1½ cups. Place the cooked spinach in a clean kitchen towel and squeeze out the excess water. In a medium bowl, stir together the cream, spinach, nutmeg, cayenne, hot sauce, and Worcestershire sauce until smooth. Season to taste with salt.

FOR THE HOLLANDAISE SAUCE: Place the vinegar, lemon juice, and egg yolks in the top of a double boiler. The water in the lower pan should be hot but not boiling. Slowly whisk until you start to see the egg yolks coagulate on the sides. Continue cooking, whisking constantly, until the yolks are lighter in color and do not leave yellow streaks when the whisk passes through them. Be sure to watch the temperature of the pan; if it gets too hot, remove it from the heat for a minute, whisking the eggs constantly. If you see any signs of scrambling, remove the pan from the heat.

When the yolk mixture is good and thick, remove from the heat and slowly drizzle in the clarified butter, whisking constantly until incorporated. Stir in the hot sauce and Worcestershire sauce, and season to taste with the salt and cayenne.

FOR THE POACHED EGGS: Line a plate with paper towels. Fill a 5-quart Dutch oven with 1 inch of water, and heat until just below a simmer. Add a few dashes of white vinegar. Crack the eggs, and gently drop them into the water, keeping the shell as close to the water as possible. With a slotted spoon, gently move the ghostlike strands of white back to the yolk. The eggs are done when the whites are no longer transparent and the yolks are still runny. Remove them onto the paper towel–lined pan with a slotted spoon and very gently dry with a towel.

FOR ASSEMBLY: Warm two plates on low in the oven. Divide the creamed spinach in the centers of the heated plates. Nestle two artichoke bottoms per plate into the spinach. Place a poached egg on each artichoke bottom, then top with a generous portion of hollandaise sauce. Sprinkle with paprika and serve.

Lake Pontchartrain

You can't leave New Orleans without taking a ride across "The Causeway," a twenty-four-mile-long bridge that crosses Lake Pontchartrain to the "Northshore." Opened in 1956, the Causeway is the longest bridge over continuous water in the world. Pontchartrain is not really a lake, but a brackish estuary that's part of one of the largest wetlands in North America. The lake is located in parts of Orleans, Jefferson, St. John the Baptist, St. Charles, St. Tammany, and Tangipahoa parishes. In Louisiana, we don't have counties like the other forty-nine states; we have parishes, and there are sixty-four in all!

Pontchartrain has long been a sportsman's paradise with abundant fish, shellfish, and waterfowl, as well as excellent access to water sports. In its heyday between 1928 and 1983, there was an area in north New Orleans on the shore of south Pontchartrain where many locals enjoyed time with their families. Pontchartrain Beach had several amusement rides, including the huge roller coaster called the Zephyr. It was quite the coaster in its time. The park also featured many famous local musicians in concert, and even Elvis headlined an act once.

⤳ Tremé Buck Jumpin' Scramble

If you've ever seen the impromptu dancing that often accompanies a parade, you'll understand why I use the term buck jumpin'.

Serves 2 to 4

4 large eggs
2 dashes Louisiana-style hot sauce
1 teaspoon Creole/Cajun spice
1 tablespoon cold water
2 tablespoons clarified butter

4 ounces Cajun Tasso (page 17)
¼ cup Holy Trinity Wit da Pope
 (page 16)
½ cup shredded sharp cheddar
 cheese

In a large bowl, combine the eggs, hot sauce, Creole/Cajun spice, and cold water, and whisk thoroughly. Melt the clarified butter in a large skillet over medium-high heat, sauté the tasso and seasoning until the onions are wilted. Reduce the heat to low, and wait a minute or 2 for the pan to cool. Add the egg mixture and stir constantly until the eggs are thoroughly cooked. Add the cheese and stir until melted. Serve immediately.

Buck Jumping

"Buck jumping" or "buck dancing" is a dance style associated with New Orleans social aid and pleasure clubs and second lines. It's usually an impromptu display that occurs during a second line parade among all-male groups. It's usually a scramble of triple-time dancing that's a mix of brass band marching and rap-influenced footwork. There is a line in the theme song to the television series *Tremé*—"The Tremé Song" by John Boutté—that refers to "buck jumping."

Second line parade

Social aid and pleasure clubs are organizations composed of different ethnic groups who organize and sponsor the second line parades for which NOLA is famous. In a typical parade, the members of the group and a grand marshal lead things off and a brass band follows, providing high energy to get the crowd involved. The term "second line" refers to the group of people that typically follows the band and actually joins the parade procession. This is seen in many funeral processions as well.

→ St. Pierre's Big Easy Crawfish Omelet

Many folks from outside Louisiana refer to these crustaceans as bait for fishing. But there's a reason Hank Williams included them in his song "Jambalaya (On the Bayou)": in NOLA they're a delicious seafood. They're really miniature lobsters, and legend has it that they're actually the descendants of lobsters who followed the boats carrying the Acadians down from Canada. It was such a long journey that they lost a lot of weight and that's why they're so tiny now.

Serves 3 to 5

1 tablespoon water
4 large egg whites
2 large whole eggs
¼ teaspoon Louisiana-style hot
  sauce
1 tablespoon chopped fresh chives
¼ cup cooked crawfish tail meat,
  chopped
1 tablespoon Creole/Cajun spice

1 teaspoon sour cream
⅓ cup sliced mushrooms
¼ cup (2 ounces) finely diced ham
  or Cajun Tasso (page 17)
2 tablespoons shredded light
  processed cheese (such as
  Velveeta)

In a medium bowl, whisk together the water, egg whites, whole eggs, hot sauce, and chives. In a second medium bowl, stir together the crawfish, Creole/Cajun spice, and sour cream.

Coat a small nonstick skillet with cooking spray and heat over medium-high heat. Add the mushrooms and ham and sauté for 3 minutes. Pour the egg mixture into the pan and cook to set slightly. Tilt the pan and carefully lift the edges of the omelet with a spatula; allow the uncooked portion to flow underneath the cooked portion. Cook for 3 minutes, then flip the omelet.

Spoon the crawfish mixture onto half of the omelet. Carefully loosen the omelet with the spatula, and fold it in half. Gently slide the omelet onto a plate and top with cheese. Cut the omelet in half and serve.

⤳ TREMEndous Oyster Omelet

You might turn your nose up on this one. Oysters and eggs? Well, I promise you, once you try this dish, you'll be longing for more. It's great for a New Orleans brunch served with a scrumptious mimosa (champagne mixed with fresh orange juice). I like to put some of my filling on top of the omelet, in addition to the butter sauce from the pan.

Serves 2 to 4

2 teaspoons bacon drippings
3 tablespoons plus 2 teaspoons
  unsalted butter, divided
6 large oysters, liqueur discarded
1 teaspoon minced garlic
2 tablespoons chopped green onions

pinch cayenne pepper
3 extra-large eggs
2 teaspoons half-and-half
1 tablespoon clarified butter or
  olive oil
sea salt

Heat a 10-inch skillet over medium-high heat. When the skillet is hot, add the bacon drippings to the pan, then add 1 tablespoon of the butter. When the butter is incorporated, add the oysters, garlic, and green onions, and sauté until the edges of the oysters curl, 1 to 2 minutes. Remove from the heat, add 2 tablespoons of the butter, and incorporate by shaking the pan. Season to taste with a bit of sea salt and the cayenne. Set aside.

In a medium bowl, whisk together the eggs, half-and-half, and a healthy pinch of sea salt. Heat a second 10-inch skillet over medium heat, add the clarified butter or olive oil, and when very hot, add the egg mixture. Cook without stirring, but gently move the omelet aside to allow the uncooked egg to run off onto the hot skillet. When the top is still uncooked, flip the omelet, then immediately turn out onto a cutting board. Spoon the filling into the center, then fold the omelet.

→ Bojangles's Baked Florentine

This nice vegetarian egg casserole has the spice and flavorings of New Orleans.

8 large eggs, well beaten
1 cup ricotta cheese
½ cup milk
5 leaves fresh basil, chopped
2 sprigs fresh oregano
¼ teaspoon salt
¼ teaspoon black pepper

1 (10-ounce) package frozen chopped spinach (about 1¼ cups), thawed and drained well
1 cup coarsely chopped plum tomatoes
½ cup thinly sliced green onions
1 cup shredded mozzarella cheese

Preheat the oven to 325°F and butter a 15 x 10-inch baking dish. In a large bowl, whisk the eggs and ricotta cheese until just combined. Stir in the milk, basil, oregano, salt, and pepper. Fold in the spinach, tomatoes, and green onions. Spread the mixture evenly in the prepared baking dish, and top with the mozzarella cheese. Bake until a toothpick inserted in the center comes out clean, about 35 minutes.

Li'l Dizzy's: A Tremé Tradition

A super-cool place to have a flavorful breakfast or a buffet-style lunch in the Tremé is Li'l Dizzy's, located at 1500 Esplanade Avenue. This popular spot is an authentic stop for Creole soul food and people watching. You'll see local characters from the neighborhood and get a genuine sampling of life in the always interesting Tremé! In one episode of *Tremé*, Li'l Dizzy's is the restaurant where Antoinette "Toni" Burnette dipped into a bread pudding that a cop had left behind.

→ Olive It! Muffuletta Frittata

This dish was inspired by New Orleans's famous muffuletta sandwiches. The saltiness of the olive salad adds a flavorful touch to this distinctive meat-and-cheese, oven-cooked egg dish.

Serves 4

6 large eggs
2 tablespoons sour cream
¼ teaspoon salt
¼ teaspoon black pepper
½ green onion, coarsely chopped
½ teaspoon fresh oregano, minced
1 cup cubed wheat bread
2 thin slices ham, coarsely chopped
3 thin slices Genoa salami, coarsely chopped

2 thin slices provolone cheese, coarsely chopped
1 tablespoon unsalted butter
⅓ cup Italian-style deli olives, pitted and chopped
1 tablespoon pickled pepperoncini, coarsely chopped
dash Louisiana-style hot sauce

In a medium bowl, beat together the eggs, sour cream, salt, and pepper with an electric mixer on medium speed until well blended, 2 to 3 minutes. Or, whisk until well blended. Mix in the green onion, oregano, and bread cubes. Let stand for 20 minutes or covered in the refrigerator overnight.

Preheat the oven to 350°F. Mix the ham, salami, and provolone cheese into the egg mixture. Melt the butter in an 8- to 9-inch ovenproof skillet over medium heat, then add the egg mixture. Bake until the egg is fluffy and cooked, about 12 minutes. While the frittata bakes, mix the olives, pepperoncinis, and hot sauce in a small bowl to make a quick Italian-style olive salad.

When the frittata is done, slice into 4 wedges. Garnish each slice with the olive salad and serve immediately.

→ SAINTsational Savory Crêpes

As in Europe, crêpes in New Orleans are thin, delicate pancakes that are often served for dessert accompanied by fresh fruit and sprinkled with confectioners' sugar. This take on the delicious, light, French-influenced breakfast item takes the sugar out and makes a nice accompaniment to your New Orleans–style omelet.

Makes 10 to 12

2 large eggs
1½ cups milk
1½ teaspoons kosher salt
pinch cayenne pepper
2 tablespoons melted unsalted
    butter

1½ cups all-purpose flour
1 tablespoon green onions, finely
    sliced
1 tablespoon flat-leaf parsley, finely
    chopped

In a large bowl, combine the eggs, milk, salt, cayenne, butter, and flour. Mix with an immersion blender until all the lumps are gone. Stir in the green onions and parsley. Cover and refrigerate for 1 hour to allow air bubbles to lessen and prevent the crêpes from tearing.

Line a plate with parchment paper. Place a crêpe pan or a medium sauté pan over medium heat until good and hot. Coat the pan with cooking spray, and ladle in about 2 ounces of the batter, working quickly to swirl the batter in a thin layer around the bottom and partially up the sides of the pan. When the edges start to brown, carefully work a rubber spatula underneath and flip the crêpe. Cook on the second side for about 30 seconds, then remove to the parchment paper to cool. Repeat with the remaining batter.

→ Carmelita's Creole Rice Fritters (Calas)

This is a terrific way to use up leftover white rice and taste part of the history of New Orleans cuisine. Hey, if you have a quart container of rice leftover from last night's Chinese dinner, make calas for breakfast!

Makes about 6

½ cup warm water (110°F)
1 tablespoon granulated sugar
1 packet (2¼ teaspoons) active dry
   yeast
¾ cup cooked white rice
2 large eggs, beaten slightly
pinch kosher salt

¼ teaspoon ground nutmeg
½ teaspoon ground cinnamon
¼ teaspoon vanilla extract
¾ cup all-purpose flour
peanut oil, for frying
confectioners' sugar, for a heavy
   dusting

Combine the warm water and sugar in a bowl and add the yeast. Let it bloom for about 10 minutes. Stir in the rice, cover with plastic wrap, and let stand overnight at room temperature.

The next day, slightly mash the rice. Mix in the eggs, salt, nutmeg, cinnamon, vanilla, and flour. Cover and let stand for about an hour.

Heat 4 inches of peanut oil in a large cast-iron pot to 365°F. Drop heaping tablespoons of the batter in batches into the hot oil. Do not overcrowd the pot. Fry until golden brown. You might want to test the oil temperature with just a few calas before you fry a whole batch, to make sure it is not too hot. If the calas brown too quickly, the inside will be gooey. If you find the batter browning too fast (within a minute), then reduce the temperature of your oil. Stir the calas as they fry to make sure they brown evenly. Drain on paper towels and immediately dust with confectioners' sugar or maybe even some Steen's pure cane syrup.

Calas

These traditional rice fritters had for the most part faded away pre-Katrina. Originally a dish from Ghana, they were made popular in the eighteenth century when Creole women of color often sold them on the streets on their days off. Many a Creole grandmother cooked calas for communions and during Mardi Gras. After Katrina, they made a resurgence as an accompaniment to dishes created by chefs returning to the city.

Gettin' da Taste Buds Goin'

Mardi Gras is the love of life.
It is the harmonic convergence of our food, our music,
our creativity,
our eccentricity, our neighborhoods, and our joy of
living. All at once.

CHRIS ROSE, TIMES-PICAYUNE *COLUMNIST AND AUTHOR OF*
1 DEAD IN ATTIC, *A COLLECTION OF POST-KATRINA STORIES
FROM THE NEWSPAPER*

What's a meal in New Orleans without a little something to get your taste buds going? From raw oysters on the half shell to a nice seafood salad to a steaming cup of seafood gumbo, the appetizers offered in the restaurants in and around Tremé are unique and a must-have when dining out. It doesn't stop there, however. Even in the household kitchens of locals, rarely do they have dinner without some type of starter. The following recipes include appetizers, salads, gumbos, and soups that have a distinctive flare you won't find anywhere else.

Starters

America has only three cities: New York, San Francisco, and New Orleans. Everywhere else is Cleveland.

—*TENNESSEE WILLIAMS*

They don't call it the Big Easy for nothing. Dining in New Orleans is not something that you rush through and finish up in a hurry. You don't want to just jump right into your entrée—you need to ease yourself into it with a nice starter, or what some call an appetizer. Most of these are seafood-based, but I've also included some that are akin to the soul food that you might find in a Tremé restaurant or in the kitchens of the neighborhood. In addition to frying up a couple of starters, stuffing your favorite vegetable or mushroom, or baking a few oysters with that special topping, there's nothing like some fresh homemade cracklins or a little bit of hog's head cheese with crackers or crispy slices of buttered, toasted French bread to start off your Tremé-style meal. Take your time and remember to savor every smell and taste as you dine in the fashion that local New Orleanians do.

Tremé's Backstreet Cultural Museum

One of the jewels of the Tremé is the Backstreet Cultural Museum, located at 1116 Henriette Delille Street. This down-to-earth and unique museum features exhibits about the history and traditions of the African-American community in the area. You can learn a lot about Skull and Bone gangs, social aid and pleasure clubs, Mardi Gras Indians, second lines, and jazz funerals here.

→ Big Chief's Marinated Crab Claws

This traditional New Orleans delicacy will have your guests begging for more. It is very important that you find the freshest crab claws available. If you live close to an ocean, you should be able to find these delectable delights. Try to avoid crab claws that have been frozen. It is also important that you let the claws marinate for at least 9 hours in the refrigerator to make sure the spices permeate the tender meat of the claw.

Serves 3 to 6

⅓ cup minced green onions
⅓ cup minced parsley
1 rib celery, minced
1 garlic clove, minced
⅓ cup olive oil
⅓ cup zesty Italian-style salad
   dressing

2 tablespoons tarragon vinegar
1 large lemon wedge
½ cup water
dash oregano
Worcestershire sauce, as needed
1 (1-pound) container crab claws

Mix all the ingredients in a large bowl. Refrigerate for about 9 hours, stirring them a couple of times while they marinate. Serve on a plate of lettuce with a bit of the sauce in a cup in the middle. This is finger food, so dig in.

✦ Tabby's Crawfish and Corn Beignets

Beignets aren't just for your sweet tooth. This dish takes your standard beignet to a whole other level!

Serves 4 to 6

½ cup milk
½ cup water
5 tablespoons salted butter
1 ¼ cups all-purpose flour
4 large eggs
¾ pound crawfish tails, coarsely
  chopped
1 green onion, green parts only,
  finely sliced

1 tablespoon Creole/Cajun spice
1 (11-ounce) can whole-kernel
  sweet corn, drained
corn oil
¼ pound peeled crawfish tails,
  whole

Warm the milk and water in a saucepan over medium-low heat. Gradually add the butter to the saucepan 1 tablespoon at a time, stirring constantly. Bring to a boil over medium heat. Remove from the heat and gradually mix the flour into the liquid, stirring constantly with a wire whisk until smooth. Return the pan to low heat and continue stirring until the mixture no longer sticks to the side of the pan.

Remove the pan from the heat and allow it to cool for about 5 minutes. Whisk the eggs until well scrambled. Slowly pour the eggs into the liquid while stirring vigorously. Continue whisking until the batter is smooth. Pour the batter into a large glass bowl and allow it to cool for about 10 minutes. Add the coarsely chopped crawfish tails, green onion, Creole/Cajun spice, and the corn kernels to the batter and stir to incorporate. Refrigerate the batter for about 30 minutes.

Once the batter is cool to the touch, pour about 3 inches of corn oil into a deep cast-ron pot and heat to 350°F. Line a plate with paper towels. Scoop a heaping tablespoon of batter and form it into a ball around one whole peeled crawfish and roll with the palms of your hands. Make these balls until you run out of batter (there should be enough batter for 10 to 12 beignets). When the oil is hot, drop one ball into the pot and fry until medium brown, 6 to 8 minutes, turning as needed. If the oil is too hot, you might have brown beignets with a gooey center. If the first beignet looks like it is browning too fast, lower the temperature of the oil a bit. Fry the remaining beignets, being careful not to overcrowd the pot. You need to give each one a chance to brown on all sides. Drain on the paper towel–lined plate. Serve these with a nice tartar sauce or maybe even a rémoulade (see page 55).

The Mardi Gras Indians

The Mardi Gras Indians are a main story line in the *Tremé* series. Albert "Big Chief" Lambreaux is a main character on the show and depicts the struggles of many who returned to the devastation of the flooding from Katrina. He leads a major Mardi Gras Indian tribe, the Mardi Gras Indians, and you get a good idea from this plotline what goes on when the tribe is preparing for Mardi Gras and their role in the carnival.

This is a tradition in which African-American members of the wards, or neighborhoods, of NOLA, organized in what are dubbed krewes, create elaborate costumes to wear and participate in Mardi Gras and St. Joseph's Day (they have also been seen at the New Orleans Jazz and Heritage Festival). As a ceremonial institution, Mardi Gras Indians have been around since the mid-nineteenth century and have gone through several incarnations to get to where they are today. The participants make their own costumes from beads and feathers in honor of Native Americans who helped them escape slavery (hence the name "Indians"). A chief's suit can cost up to $5,000 to make. Their chants and dances have also had an influence on the music of New Orleans. For more on the history and traditions of this group, visit the website www.mardigrasindians.com. While in the city you can visit the Backstreet Cultural Museum at 1116 St. Claude Street in the heart of Tremé, where the history and costumes are displayed.

✦ Blue Tarp Blues Fried Green Tomatoes with Shrimp Rémoulade

This is a NOLA take on the traditional Southern treat. Rémoulade is a classic Creole sauce. You can use boiled, sautéed, or fried shrimp for this dish. If you were eating them in Tremé, chances are they would be fried.

Serves 2

RÉMOULADE
½ cup mayonnaise
2 tablespoons Creole mustard
2 tablespoons ketchup
2 teaspoons cream-style horseradish
2 small garlic cloves
2 tablespoons freshly squeezed lemon juice
2 teaspoons capers, drained and rinsed
2 green onions, chopped
½ teaspoon cayenne pepper
½ teaspoon paprika
hot sauce, as needed

FRIED GREEN TOMATOES
peanut oil
1 cup corn flour
2 large eggs, lightly beaten
1 cup cornmeal
2 tablespoons Creole/Cajun spice
2 large green tomatoes, sliced ¼ inch thick (about 8 slices)

ASSEMBLY
2 cups cole slaw salad mix
16 boiled, sautéed, or fried peeled jumbo shrimp
1 batch cold rémoulade sauce

TO MAKE THE RÉMOULADE: Blend all the ingredients until smooth. Refrigerate for 2 hours.

TO MAKE THE FRIED GREEN TOMATOES: Pour about 2 inches of peanut oil into a cast-iron frying pan and heat to 375°F. Place the corn flour, eggs, and cornmeal in three separate shallow bowls. Season the corn flour and cornmeal with 1 tablespoon each of the Creole/Cajun spice. Dredge the tomato slices in the corn flour, then dip them in the egg, and finally dredge them in the cornmeal. Fry the tomato slices until golden brown on both sides, 1 to 2 minutes per side.

TO ASSEMBLE: Plate 4 cold dishes with a layer of cole slaw mix and ladle about 2 tablespoons of sauce over the slaw. Place 2 green tomatoes on each dish and then top with 4 shrimp. Top each shrimp with about 1 tablespoon of rémoulade sauce.

✦ Miss Gladiola's Big Easy Cracklins

In New Orleans, you'll often hear locals say, "Those cracklins fresh out of the grease is some fine eatin'!" These ain't the pork rinds you buy at da store!

Serves 4

2 pounds pork rind or skin
sea salt

2 pounds lard (or 1 quart
vegetable oil)
black pepper

Preheat the oven to 250°F. Cut the pork rind or skin into 2-inch squares. Spread in a single layer on a rimmed baking sheet and sprinkle with the salt. Bake for 3 hours. Cool and set aside.

Line a baking sheet with paper towels. Melt the lard (or pour the oil) to about one-third the depth of a large cast-iron Dutch oven over medium-high heat. Heat to 365°F. Fry the pork rinds or skin until they puff up and are crispy. Drain on the paper towel–lined baking sheet and serve with a dash of black pepper.

✦ Big O's Oysters Batiste

These are in the tradition of Oysters Rockefeller, created at New Orleans's famous Antoine's restaurant around 1899. Oysters are an infamous aphrodisiac—this recipe will get your motor running.

Serves 4

24 freshly shucked medium to large
oysters, patted dry
¼ cup (½ stick) unsalted butter
2 tablespoons minced shallots
3 tablespoons freshly squeezed
lemon juice

salt and cayenne pepper
8 canned artichoke hearts, drained
and chopped
½ cup Italian-style breadcrumbs
¼ cup freshly grated Parmesan
cheese

Preheat the oven to 375°F. Arrange the oysters in a single layer in a shallow baking dish. Heat the butter in a medium skillet over medium heat. Add the shallots and cook, stirring, until just soft, 1 to 2 minutes. Add the lemon juice, and season to taste with salt and cayenne pepper. Pour the mixture evenly among the oysters. Scatter the chopped artichokes over the oysters, and sprinkle with the breadcrumbs and Parmesan cheese. Bake until heated through, about 20 minutes. Serve hot with toasted, sliced French bread.

→ YEZZINDEED Crab Nachos

This NOLA take on nachos combines a Mexican-style dish with locally harvested crabmeat. They are also delicious made with peeled medium shrimp or crawfish tails instead of the crab.

8 ounces (1 cup) sour cream
4 tablespoons mayonnaise
8 sprigs cilantro, leaves only, chopped
2 green onions, green parts only, thinly sliced
2 tablespoons Tabasco Jalapeño Pepper Sauce
1 teaspoon freshly squeezed lime juice

¼ teaspoon salt
pinch cayenne pepper
40 large thick blue corn tortilla chips, or other tortilla chips
1 pound fresh or packaged lump, white, or claw crabmeat (remove all shell fragments)
1 cup shredded Asiago cheese

Place a shelf in the middle of the oven, and preheat the oven to 400°F. In a large bowl, stir together the sour cream, mayonnaise, cilantro, green onions, Tabasco sauce, lime juice, salt, and cayenne pepper to combine well. Transfer the mixture to a squeeze bottle with a large opening at the tip.

Arrange as many tortilla chips as will fit on a pizza pan, and squeeze about ⅛ teaspoon of the sauce mixture onto each chip. Top each chip with about 1 tablespoon of crabmeat. Squeeze another teaspoon of the sauce over the crab, and top each one with about 1 teaspoon of the Asiago cheese.

Bake until the cheese begins to melt, about 2 minutes. Remove from the oven and serve immediately.

Growing Latin Influences in NOLA Cuisine

Many folks don't realize that there is a strong Latin influence in New Orleans. This influence has grown exponentially since Hurricane Katrina, when the need for workers to help with restoration attracted a large influx of migrant workers from Mexico and other Latin American countries. This growing Latino population has brought with it cultural influences, including Latin American architecture, the growth of food trucks for inexpensive and delicious street food, and evidence of south-of-the-border twists on traditional NOLA recipes.

✧ Shannon's Cheese Straws

These cheese straws, a common finger food at cocktail parties in the Crescent City, are named in honor of Shannon Powell, "The King of Tremé." He's an American jazz and New Orleans jazz virtuoso drummer who is featured in the *Tremé* theme song. More information on his music can be found at his website, www.thekingoftreme.com. These snacks are a yummy must-have for your Tremé-inspired get-togethers.

Serves 4 to 6

¾ cup all-purpose flour
1 ¼ cups shredded good-quality
  sharp cheddar cheese
¼ cup (½ stick) unsalted butter,
  at room temperature, cut into
  ½-inch cubes

1 large egg yolk, beaten
½ teaspoon cayenne pepper
1 teaspoon salt
1 teaspoon black pepper

Preheat the oven to 400°F. In a large bowl, blend the flour and cheese using your hands. Rub in the butter, and then work in the egg yolk, cayenne pepper, salt, and pepper. Knead the dough for a few minutes until it is a nice shiny ball. On a floured surface, roll out the ball with a rolling pin to a thickness of ⅓ inch and cut into 2-inch strips with a knife. Arrange the strips on an ungreased baking sheet. Bake until golden orange, 15 to 20 minutes. Let cool. These can be stored in an airtight container for several days.

→ Just North of the Quarter Hog's Head Cheese

This prepared pork item is popular throughout south Louisiana and has its origins in both the butcher shops of NOLA and in the swamps of Cajun country. This version assumes you don't have any hog heads lying around and calls for pork neck bones, but if you can find jowl meat (the cheek), that would be closer to the traditional version. Check with your local grocer or butcher shop (especially an Asian or Latin American one) for the jowls.

Serves 8 to 10

6 fresh pig's feet
6 pounds pork neck
2 large onions, minced
½ head garlic, minced

1 cup water
1 tablespoon minced green onion,
  green tops only
1 tablespoon chopped parsley

In a large stockpot, boil the pig's feet and pork neck until tender, 20 to 30 minutes. Remove all bones. In a small saucepan, simmer the onions and garlic in the water until tender, about 8 minutes. Transfer the mixture to the stockpot containing the meat, add the green onions and parsley, and stir. Cook over high heat until the water has boiled off. Pour into 5-inch round bowls and allow to congeal. Serve with your favorite crackers or freshly baked slices of French bread.

Head Cheese

Head cheese, often referred to as "souse meat" or simply "souse," is not a cheese at all, but a gelatinous pork meat product. Traditionally it was made by boiling the head of an animal with all the organs (brain, eyes, ears, and so on) removed, and then simmering it and letting it cool until the fats congeal. The Louisiana version of head cheese is highly seasoned and is often used as a cold cut or appetizer.

In recent years, in keeping with the slow food movement and its emphasis on local foods and traditional techniques, dishes such as head cheese have seen a revival as chefs have become more interested in cooking with the whole animal. To taste a Southern take on these techniques, try out Cochon, a popular restaurant on Tchoupitoulas Street just east of the Central Business District (aka the CBD), south of the Quarter in the Warehouse District, where they have taken charcuterie to a whole new level of Cajun and Southern cuisine.

⇒ Salads

The culture of New Orleans is like a big head of lettuce.
You have to peel back each layer.
New Orleans culture is not one thing but a mixture of many things.
I still don't have it figured out yet.

—*DR. MICHAEL WHITE, NEW ORLEANS JAZZ CLARINETIST, BANDLEADER, COMPOSER, JAZZ HISTORIAN, AND MUSICAL EDUCATOR*

Salads are great on those hot, steamy summer afternoons when you just don't want to eat anything too heavy, and during a larger meal they bridge the gap and cleanse the palate between courses. Why not have it after you've had your starter or a bowl of gumbo or soup? Nothing helps to prolong the dining experience than to add a small salad to your meal. And after all, isn't that what eating is supposed to be? Slow and easy.

St. Augustine Church

The historically beautiful and architecturally stunning St. Augustine Church, at 1210 Gov. Nicholls Street in the Tremé, was established by free people of color in 1842. St. Augustine is one of the oldest African-American Catholic churches in the United States. Each year, during Satchmo Fest (named for famed NOLA trumpeter Louis "Satchmo" Armstrong), they have a rather high-spirited and entirely fascinating Jazz Mass. The church is also the site of the Tomb of the Unknown Slave, which honors the many slaves who were buried in unmarked graves in the Tremé and throughout North America.

Tomb of the Unknown Slave

✈ Antoinette's Shrimp Salad

I can imagine this as a lunch item when Antoinette "Toni" Bernette, a character on the series *Tremé*, is having lunch with the DA or Lieutenant Colson. It also makes a nice transition between your starter, gumbo, or soup and your entrée.

¼ cup freshly squeezed lemon juice
3 tablespoons capers, drained
1 medium shallot, minced
1 tablespoon Creole mustard
½ teaspoon crushed red pepper
½ cup olive oil
½ cup chopped fresh basil
2 pounds uncooked large shrimp,
   peeled and deveined

2 zucchini, cut into ½-inch cubes
   (about 2 cups)
8 cups mixed baby greens (about 5
   ounces)
freshly grated Parmesan cheese
salt and black pepper

Whisk together the lemon juice, capers, shallot, mustard, and crushed red pepper in a medium bowl. Whisk in the oil, then the basil. Season the dressing with salt and black pepper to taste.

Bring a large saucepan of salted water to a boil. Add the shrimp and cook for 1 minute. Add the zucchini, and continue cooking until the shrimp are opaque in the center and the zucchini is crisp-tender, about 1 minute longer. Drain, rinse under cold water, and let cool. Transfer to a large bowl and add ⅓ cup of the dressing and toss to coat. Taste, and adjust the seasoning with salt and pepper as needed.

Toss the greens in a large bowl with enough of the remaining dressing to coat. Divide the greens among 4 plates. Arrange the shrimp and zucchini atop the greens and sprinkle with Parmesan cheese.

→ Epiphany's Pasta Salad with Shrimp

This makes for a healthy full meal, too. Make a batch and graze on it for a couple of days. You can also substitute gluten-free noodles if you don't handle wheat well.

Serves 4 to 8

1 pound uncooked medium shrimp, peeled and deveined
1 (12-ounce) bag rainbow rotini pasta
2 large cucumbers, peeled and cubed
3 ribs celery, sliced

2 large tomatoes, cubed
½ cup mayonnaise
1 (1-ounce) package prepared ranch dressing mix
1 tablespoon Creole/Cajun spice

Bring a large pot of salted water to a boil. After the water has boiled for about 2 minutes, add the shrimp and cook until they turn pink, about 2 minutes. Remove with a slotted spoon and set aside. Using the same pot of boiling water, cook the pasta according to the package directions, stirring frequently. Drain, let cool slightly, and transfer to a large bowl.

Add the shrimp, cucumbers, celery, and tomatoes to the pasta and toss together. Then add the mayonnaise and ranch dressing mix, and stir to combine well. Season with the Creole/Cajun spice. Cover and refrigerate for about 2 hours so all the flavors can set. Serve cold.

Creole Tomatoes

One sure-fire way to make friends with your neighbors is to give them a gift of Creole tomatoes right off the vine. New Orleanians are very proud of the meaty, juicy, and thick red Creole tomatoes that we wait for every summer. They also usually have crowns—proof that they're tomato royalty! We grow them in our backyards and patio pots, and we eagerly await that first batch of glorious vine-ripened Creole tomatoes. In fact, we are so proud of our signature tomato that there's even a Creole Tomato Festival in the heart of the French Quarter each June. We swear by their superior flavor and credit the rich soil of our region for their deliciousness. Starting in early June, Creole tomatoes can be bought at roadside stands, farmer's markets, and urban grocery stores throughout the greater New Orleans area.

→ Robicheaux's Yeah, U Right Crawfish Salad with Creole Honey-Mustard Dressing

Legendary blues artist and colorful NOLA character Coco Robicheaux made a cameo appearance in the second episode of the series *Tremé*. Unfortunately, we lost this legendary blues artist in November 2011 at the age of 64. He released his album *Yeah, U Rite!* in 2005 and followed it up in 2008 with *Like I Said, Yeah, U Rite!* You'll hear this phrase used often on the streets of Tremé. It's used to strongly agree with something that someone says to you.

Serves 4

 DRESSING

6 tablespoons Creole mustard

1½ tablespoons freshly squeezed lemon juice

1½ tablespoons honey

1 teaspoon Suck da Heads and Pinch da Tails Creole Spice (page 13)

1 teaspoon olive oil

 SALAD

6 cups thinly sliced romaine lettuce

3¾ cups sliced mushrooms

2 cups cooked crawfish tail meat (about 12 ounces)

⅓ cup sliced green onions

¼ cup sliced roasted red bell peppers (jarred are fine)

2 tablespoons sunflower seed kernels, toasted

1 (2¼-ounce) can sliced ripe black olives, drained

1 large hard-cooked egg, sliced

TO MAKE THE DRESSING: In a small bowl, whisk all the ingredients to combine.

TO MAKE THE SALAD: Combine all the ingredients in a large bowl. Add the dressing, and toss well.

→ Lambreaux's Strawberry-Asparagus Salad

This one might be a favorite of Delmond Lambreaux, the character on HBO's *Tremé* who had problems with the traditions of his father and the city. This recipe is different from the rich dishes that are associated with NOLA cuisine, giving a light alternative to the usual heavy sauces and fried fare of the region. Asparagus is not native to the Deep South, but the strawberries give it a south Louisiana distinction.

 Serves 4

 ¼ cup freshly squeezed lemon juice
2 tablespoons olive oil
2 tablespoons honey

2 cups fresh asparagus, cut into
1-inch pieces (about 1 pound)
2 cups sliced fresh strawberries

In a small bowl, whisk together the lemon juice, olive oil, and honey. Prepare an ice bath by filling a large bowl with water and ice. Bring a small amount of water to a boil in a saucepan. Add the asparagus and cook until crisp-tender, 3 to 4 minutes. Drain, and immediately plunge into the ice bath, which will help preserve the vegetable's green color. Arrange the asparagus and strawberries on individual plates, and drizzle with the dressing.

✵ Soups and Gumbos

"I'm not going to lay down in words the lure of this place. Every great writer in the land, from Faulkner to Twain to Rice to Ford, has tried to do it and fallen short. It is impossible to capture the essence, tolerance, and spirit of south Louisiana in words and to try is to roll down a road of clichés, bouncing over beignets and beads and brass bands and it just is what it is. It is home."

—*CHRIS ROSE, AUTHOR OF 1 DEAD IN ATTIC*

Gumbo is the all-time favorite comfort dish down here, but remember, we don't throw gumbo parties. However, Sunday is known as "gumbo day"! And cold weather is often referred to as "gumbo weather."

To me, gumbo is a marvelous middle-ground between stew and soup. Sometimes it's chunky, with Cajun-style smoked sausage and chicken, or sometimes it's filled with plump Gulf shrimp and lump blue crab. A warm bowl of steaming gumbo satisfies the soul during damp, cold, and windy Tremé winters. In south Louisiana gumbo is more like a primary food group!

Making genuine gumbo the traditional way may not be the best strategy for some "fast food" cooks, but it's OK to cheat too—just buy a pre-packaged gumbo mix (some of them are actually pretty good).

New Orleans cuisine is also known for its thick and hardy bisques, French onion soup, and tomato-based soups. I've included my favorite recipe for each.

Filé Gumbo

Most Tremé folks know that the word gumbo is African in origin and actually means "okra"; indeed, some insist that if it doesn't contain okra, it isn't really gumbo. Traditionally, a gumbo without okra would have filé powder sprinkled over each individual serving and would be called filé gumbo. Filé powder works as a flavoring and thickening agent in the stew and can be found in most grocery stores in the spice section. Personally, I like to add a little filé powder even when my gumbo already has okra in it, because I think it makes it taste even better! To each their own. The rules are yours to make or break!

→ Robertson Street Green Onion Soup

New Orleans's strong French influences make for amazing French onion soup, and you'll find it is served in most NOLA restaurants. This recipe takes a different approach from the traditional broth with croutons and melted cheese on top.

Serves 4

4 tablespoons unsalted butter
6 bunches green onions
5 cups vegetable broth
2 cups white mushrooms, sliced

⅓ cup heavy cream
salt and black pepper
hot French bread, to serve

Melt the butter in a large stockpot over medium heat, and add the onions and some salt and pepper. Sauté until the onions are translucent, 3 to 4 minutes, then add the broth and bring the mixture to a boil over high heat. Reduce the heat to low, cover the pan, and let the soup simmer for 10 minutes. Add 1 cup of the mushrooms and purée the soup in a blender or food processor until smooth. Put the soup back in the pot, and stir in the cream and the remaining 1 cup of mushrooms. Cook gently over medium-low heat until the mushrooms are tender. Serve hot with French bread slathered in butter.

→ Cousin Trosclair's Creole Tomato Soup

The subtle seasonings and chunks of smoky sausage in this quick, easy, and delicious soup make it taste as flavorful as any long-simmered soup.

Serves 4 to 8

1 tablespoon vegetable oil
1 cup finely chopped yellow onion
1 cup finely chopped celery
½ cup finely chopped yellow bell pepper
1 garlic clove, minced
1 (28-ounce) can diced tomatoes
1 (14-ounce) can chicken broth
1 teaspoon dried thyme

⅛ teaspoon cayenne pepper
1 bay leaf
1 (7-ounce) link precooked andouille sausage, finely chopped (about 1½ cups)
3 tablespoons half-and-half or heavy cream (optional)
warm corn muffins, to serve

Heat the vegetable oil in a large, heavy saucepan over medium heat until hot. Add the onion, celery, bell pepper, and garlic and cook, stirring often, until softened, about 6 minutes. Add the tomatoes, broth, thyme, cayenne pepper, and bay leaf. Increase the heat to high, and bring to a boil. Reduce the heat to medium-low, and simmer until the vegetables are soft, 20 to 25 minutes. Add the sausage and cook until heated through, about 1 minute. Remove from the heat. Remove and discard the bay leaf, and stir in the half-and-half or heavy cream, if using. Serve hot with warm corn muffins.

Voilà, y'all!

Zulu Mardi Gras Krewe

The Zulu Social Aid and Pleasure Club was founded in 1916. It's a Carnival Krewe in New Orleans and the largest predominantly African-American Carnival organization in the city. Each year the Zulu parade rolls on Fat Tuesday, or Mardi Gras Day. Zulu is known for its unique throw of hand-painted coconuts. In 1988, the city forbade the Krewe from throwing coconuts due to the risk of injury; these days, they are handed to on-looking paradegoers rather than tossed.

→ Davis McAlary's Crab and Corn Soup

This soup is the chowder of New Orleans. It's robust and will fill you up quick and stick to your ribs.

Serves 4

kernels from 8 ears corn
1 quart (4 cups) chicken broth,
    divided
2 tablespoons unsalted butter
1 medium white onion, chopped
¼ cup dry white wine
1½ teaspoons sea salt

1½ cups milk
½ pound fresh or packaged lump
    crabmeat (remove all shell
    fragments)
⅓ cup chopped green onion, green
    parts only

In a blender or food processor, combine half the corn and 2 cups of the broth. Pulse to a coarse purée.

In a large pot, melt the butter over low heat. Add the onion and cook until translucent, stirring occasionally, for 5 minutes. Add the corn purée, the other half of the corn, the wine, the remaining 2 cups of broth, and the salt to the pot.

Increase the heat to high and bring to a boil. Reduce the heat to low and simmer until the corn is tender, about 15 minutes. Add the milk and return to a simmer. Stir in the crabmeat and green onions. Serve hot.

✦ Xenora's Gumbo Z'Herbes

This quintessential Creole dish is also known as "green gumbo." The tradition behind gumbo z'herbes is that it was generally cooked on Holy Thursday to eat on Good Friday. Leave out the ham hocks for a tasty vegetarian version.

Serves 12

2½ quarts (10 cups) water
8 to 10 cabbage leaves
8 ounces mustard greens (about 1 bunch)
8 ounces turnip greens (about 1 bunch)
8 ounces beet greens (from about 1 bunch beets)
2 (1-pound) smoked ham hocks
1 tablespoon unsalted butter
3 cups Holy Trinity Wit da Pope (page 16)
2 tablespoons all-purpose flour

2 tablespoons fresh or 1 tablespoon dried thyme
2 small fresh hot red chilies, minced, seeds included for more heat
8 ounces fresh baby spinach
¼ cup chopped fresh parsley
4 tablespoons apple cider vinegar
All That Jazz Creole and Cajun Blast (page 14), as needed
Louisiana-style hot sauce, to serve
hot rice or corn bread, to serve

Bring the water to a boil in an 8-quart pot over high heat. Add the cabbage and simmer over low heat, covered, until cabbage is limp, about 10 minutes. Remove the cabbage with a slotted spoon and set aside.

Add 4 ounces each of the mustard greens, turnip greens, and beet greens to the water the cabbage was cooked in, and simmer, uncovered, over low heat for about 7 minutes. Remove the greens with a slotted spoon and set aside. Repeat with the remaining 4 ounces of each green. When the greens have cooled down enough, finely chop them.

Add the ham hocks to the liquid the greens were cooked in, and simmer, covered, over medium-low heat for 50 minutes. Remove with a slotted spoon and place on a cutting board to cool. When cool enough to handle, discard the bones and skin, and finely chop the ham. Pour the cooking liquid into a large bowl, adding water as needed to equal 5 cups total.

Melt the butter in the pot over medium-low heat, then add the Holy Trinity Wit da Pope and cook, stirring frequently, until golden, about 6 minutes. Add the flour and cook, stirring, for 4 minutes.

Slowly add the reserved cooking liquid, stirring constantly. Add all the cooked, chopped greens and the thyme, chilies, and ham, and simmer, uncovered, until the greens are tender, about 10 minutes.

Add the spinach and stir until wilted. Stir in the parsley, vinegar, and Creole seasoning. Serve hot with your favorite hot sauce and rice or cornbread.

⤳ Iberville Creole Gumbo

Gumbos are Cajun or Creole soups or stews that come in all shapes and sizes and contain a variety of meats and, quite frequently, okra, an African vegetable for which gumbo is named. Gumbos are often served over rice. This one is made from a simple recipe, and I guarantee you'll want seconds.

Serves 4

2½ cups water
4 bone-in, skin-on chicken breast
  halves
8 bone-in, skin-on chicken thighs
3 cups Holy Trinity (page 16)
½ cup all-purpose flour
½ cup unsalted butter

1 pound andouille sausage
1 pound uncooked medium to large
  shrimp, peeled and deveined
1½ tablespoons In the Mix Gumbo
  Spice (page 14)
white rice, to serve
French bread, to serve

In a 12-quart pot, bring the water to a boil and add the chicken and the Holy Trinity and boil until the chicken is completely cooked through, 30 to 45 minutes. Remove the chicken from the pot and reserve the water and the Holy Trinity.

In an 8-quart cast-iron Dutch oven over medium heat, stir together the flour and butter to make a dark brown roux (see page 20). When the roux is done, combine the chicken, sausage, and the reserved water to the pot and bring to a boil over medium-high heat. Reduce the heat to medium-low, cover the pan, and simmer for about 1 hour. Add the shrimp and simmer for about 20 minutes longer. Stir in gumbo spice mix and serve hot over white rice. French bread is a must with gumbo to sop up the juices.

Nothing Goes to Waste in NOLA

In the Tremé neighborhood, families have always done everything they could to make their food stretch and to prevent food from being thrown away, a tradition that is still in practice today. There are many recipes that were made with leftover ingredients. Pain perdu and the quintessential dessert bread pudding were favorite ways to use up stale bread. Leftover rice was also often made into a pudding. Succotash and goulash were commonly cooked in Tremé with leftover vegetables from a supper. Of course, the ultimate solution to preventing food waste is a big old pot of gumbo made with everything but the kitchen sink.

→ Gentilly Seafood Filé Gumbo

Gentilly is a mostly middle-class and racially diverse area of New Orleans located on Lake Pontchartrain east of City Park. Home to the University of New Orleans main campus and Dillard University, and not far from the fairgrounds, Gentilly was badly damaged following Hurricane Katrina. Gentilly's population has slowly returned. In honor of the area's resilience, I named this delicious gumbo Gentilly. The fish for this dish should be a firm variety so that it doesn't fall apart. I suggest a white, lean, and firm fish such as pollock, grouper, haddock, cod, or halibut. Of course, we use catfish in Louisiana.

Serves 10 to 20

1 cup vegetable oil
1 cup all-purpose flour
3 cups Holy Trinity Wit da Pope
  (page 16)
8 cups seafood or chicken stock,
  canned or from bouillon base
2 (28-ounce) cans tomatoes, diced
2 (10-ounce) packages frozen
  thawed and sliced okra
1 pound crab claws
¼ cup Worcestershire sauce
1 tablespoon hot sauce
2 large bay leaves
½ cup fresh minced parsley
2 teaspoons dried thyme

2 teaspoons dried basil
2 teaspoons dried oregano
1 teaspoon dried sage
1 teaspoon black pepper
2 pounds medium shrimp, peeled
  and deveined
1 quart large oysters, liqueur
  reserved
1 pound fresh or packaged lump
  crabmeat (remove all shell
  fragments)
1 pound firm fish fillets, cut in
  1-inch pieces
hot cooked white rice, to serve
filé powder (optional)

In a large, heavy skillet (cast-iron works best) over medium heat, combine the oil and flour to make a roux (see page 20). Cook, stirring constantly, until the roux is dark brown, about the color of milk chocolate. Be very careful to keep the roux from scorching. Stir in the Holy Trinity Wit da Pope and sauté, stirring often, until the vegetables are translucent, about 10 minutes.

Transfer the mixture to a large stockpot. Add the chicken stock, tomatoes, okra, crab claws, Worcestershire sauce, hot sauce, bay leaves, parsley, thyme, basil, oregano, sage, and pepper. Stir well and bring to a boil over high heat. Reduce the heat and simmer for 2 hours, stirring occasionally.

Add the shrimp, oysters and their liqueur, crabmeat, and fish to the pot, and simmer until the shrimp turn pink, 10 to 15 minutes. Remove and discard the bay leaves. Serve hot over hot cooked rice and sprinkle with filé powder, if desired.

The Rebirth Brass Band

The Rebirth Brass Band is my favorite New Orleans band. The group was founded in 1982 by tuba/sousaphone player Philip Frazier; his brother, bass drummer Keith Frazier; and trumpeter Kermit Ruffins; along with other school marching band members from Joseph S. Clark Senior High School in the Tremé neighborhood. The band was discovered at the 1982 New Orleans Jazz and Heritage Festival and recorded its first studio album in 1984.

After Hurricane Katrina, Rebirth started playing again on Tuesday nights at the Maple Leaf, which was important on myriad levels to the Big Easy nightlife scene. Things were getting back to normal, returning slowly to the pre-storm days and ways. Having Rebirth play again felt like an important milestone, like the return of the Fais Do Do at Tipitina's on Sunday afternoons or the Mid-City Lanes zydeco stomp each Thursday night. Something predictable, good, and right! It dawned on me—yeah, we are getting our rhythm back! A veteran of NOLA's music

Maple Leaf Bar

renaissance, Rebirth Brass Band symbolizes so many unspoken things about the region to us natives. Much, much more than just a marching band, they are the melody of Mardi Gras, wild street parades, festive second-lines, and the best house parties. To put it plainly—they just sound like home!

In the first episode of *Tremé*, Elvis Costello hires Rebirth during his recording sessions with Allen Toussaint. In real life, Costello spent a lot of time in the city, and the recording with Toussaint actually took place. Their collaboration produced the song "The River in Reverse" on one of the first albums recorded in the city after the storm. It was inspirational to local musicians and is attributed to a revitalization of the music scene.

→ Where Y'at? Shredded Pork Gumbo with Black-Eyed Peas

The phrase "Where y'at?" is a common greeting around Tremé and in the greater New Orleans area in general. It's like simultaneously saying, "Where are you?" and "How are you?" with just two small words! Who Dat Potato Salad (page 90) goes great with this gumbo.

Serves 15 to 20

1 cup all-purpose flour
1 cup canola oil
3 cups Holy Trinity Wit da Pope (page 16)
1½ gallons (24 cups) unsalted pork or chicken stock
4 slices thick-cut bacon
1 (16-ounce) bag cooked frozen collard or mustard greens, unthawed
1 (16-ounce) bag of cooked frozen okra, unthawed and sliced

2 (15½-ounce) cans black-eyed peas
2 pounds shredded smoked pork butt
1 teaspoon Louisiana-style hot sauce
1 tablespoon vinegar
1 tablespoon sugar
In the Mix Gumbo Spice (page 14)
hot rice and fresh French bread, to serve

In an 8-quart Dutch oven or stockpot, use the flour and oil to make a chocolate brown roux (see page 20). Sauté the Holy Trinity Wit da Pope in the roux until the vegetables are translucent. Add the pork or chicken stock to the pot and bring to a boil. Simmer for 1 hour.

Fry the bacon in a skillet over medium-high heat until crispy. Remove the bacon and set aside. Sauté the greens, okra, peas, and pork until the okra is cooked. When the gumbo has simmered for 1 hour, crumble the bacon into the sautéed vegetables and stir in the hot sauce, vinegar, and sugar. Add this to the gumbo pot. Add the In the Mix Gumbo Spice and simmer for 15 minutes longer. Serve with rice and fresh French bread.

⇥ Side Dishes

"Clean living keeps me in shape. Righteous thoughts are my secret. And New Orleans home cooking."

—*FATS DOMINO*

Some of the unique and delectable side dishes commonly served in the Tremé neighborhood of New Orleans are part of what makes a meal here a complete experience. All segments combine to give you one magical culinary encounter. Sometimes the side dishes are so outstanding they actually upstage the main dish. Come visit the Tremé and you'll understand what I'm sayin', doll!

Makin' Groceries

In episode 12 of the *Tremé* series on HBO, "Everthing I Do Gonh Be Funky," Desirée (Antoine Batiste's baby-momma) mentions that she has groceries to make. "Makin' groceries" is an old south Louisiana expression that the region's residents use for food shopping. The expression derives from the French phrase *faire son marché*, "to do one's market shopping"; faire translates as either "to do" or "to make." My very Cajun-Frenchy Maw-Maw would always say, "I need to go make groceries," and us kids would get such a laugh out of that old phrase!

✦ Creole Wedding Rings

Many married couples in the region eat this dish on their anniversary to enhance passion and preserve fidelity. Casting a food-spell is one way to ensure one's partner in life is faithful!

Serves 8 to 12

6 large red onions
¼ cup (½ stick) unsalted butter
2 whole cloves

½ teaspoon garlic salt
¼ teaspoon black pepper
1 cup Burgundy wine

Cut the onions into ¼-inch slices and separate into rings. Melt the butter in a large skillet over medium heat. Add the onions and stir until well coated. Add the cloves, garlic salt, and pepper, and sauté until the onions start to become soft, 5 to 8 minutes. Add the wine, cover, and simmer about 15 minutes over low heat. Uncover the pan and discard the cloves. Continue to cook, uncovered, until the liquid is reduced almost to a glaze. This can be eaten over rice or used as a relish with a dish.

✦ Hildago's Dirty Rice

This Cajun dish gets it name from the chicken livers and gizzards that produce what look to be specks of dirt in the rice. Also known as rice dressing, it's served as an accompaniment to seafood dishes or as an entrée. In the series *Tremé*, Hildago is a Dallas businessman who characterizes many of the dirty vultures who came to the city to capitalize on the opportunities that were available after Katrina. These buzzards milked a lot of money from a city that couldn't afford it at the time.

Serves 8

½ pound ground beef
5 chicken livers, chopped
5 chicken gizzards, chopped
salt and cayenne pepper
1 tablespoon Creole/Cajun spice

1 tablespoon unsalted butter
1 cup parsley, chopped
1½ cups green onions, chopped
2 cups white rice
4½ cups chicken broth

Season the beef, livers, and gizzards with salt, cayenne pepper, and the Creole/Cajun spice. Melt the butter in a large skillet over medium heat, and add the meat to the pan. Increase the heat to medium-high heat, and cook, stirring to crumble, until the beef is browned. Add the parsley and green onion, and cook, stirring occasionally, until the vegetables are softened, about 8 minutes. Stir in the rice and add the broth. Bring to a boil, cover, reduce the heat to low, and simmer for 1 hour. Sprinkle the surface of the rice with black pepper before serving.

→ Bountiful Harvest Bourbon Sweet Potatoes

You've had sweet potatoes prepared as a casserole like this if you were born and raised in the South. The bourbon in this version adds a distinct flavor to the dish. For more flavor, add more bourbon! (Oh, and it's OK to have a nip or two when you are throwing this together.)

4 (1-pound) cans sweet potato or
   yams in liquid
1 cup sugar
¼ cup unsalted butter
¼ cup bourbon

heavy cream, as needed
½ cup chopped pecans
1 (12-ounce) bag mini
   marshmallows

Preheat the oven to 350°F and butter a 15 x 10-inch casserole dish. In a large saucepan, heat the sweet potatoes or yams and their liquid over medium heat. Drain and gently mash 'em up, leaving a few lumps. Stir in the sugar, butter, bourbon, and enough cream to achieve the consistency of mashed potatoes. Spread the mixture evenly in the prepared dish, and sprinkle the pecans on top. Bake until bubbling, about 30 minutes. Cover the top with the marshmallows, and return to the oven to brown, about 15 minutes. Watch closely to make sure the marshmallows don't burn.

Lagniappe

Often translated as "a little something extra," lagniappe (LAN-yap) is a phrase you'll often hear in south Louisiana. It's similar to a baker's dozen, when a thirteenth donut might be added to a dozen as a courtesy to the customer. This is a common practice among street vendors in Louisiana, where the expectation is that they will throw a few extra in with your order. You will also find this among oyster shuckers, who should always throw on a thirteenth oyster to your dozen on the half shell.

→ Grandma Shoog's Fried Cabbage with Bacon, Onion, and Garlic

Cabbage is a staple in Southern kitchens, but in south Louisiana we don't just boil it with some bland meat. We cook it with bacon, seasonings, and spices and let it make its own juices. "Shoog" is common vernacular in the NOLA area and is short for "sugar," as in, "How ya doin', Shoog?" This dish goes great with pork or beef roast.

Serves 4 to 8

6 slices bacon, chopped
1 large yellow onion, diced
2 garlic cloves, minced
1 large head cabbage, cored and
   sliced

1 tablespoon salt, or as needed
1 teaspoon black pepper
½ teaspoon onion powder
½ teaspoon garlic powder
⅛ teaspoon paprika

In a large stockpot over medium-high heat, cook the bacon until crispy, about 10 minutes. Add the onion and garlic, and cook, stirring, until the onion caramelizes, about 10 minutes. Immediately stir in the cabbage and continue to cook, stirring, for 10 minutes longer. Stir in the salt, pepper, onion powder, garlic powder, and paprika. Reduce the heat to low, cover, and simmer, stirring occasionally, about 30 minutes more.

→ Swamp Opal's Oyster Dressing

Often called stuffing outside of the south, this cornbread and oyster dressing can be served as an alternative to the more traditional basic cornbread dressing that is often served with turkey. Thanksgiving and Christmas in New Orleans wouldn't be holidays without oyster dressing. It is YUUUUUMMYYY!

Serves 10 to 15

 turkey neck, gizzard, heart, and
   liver from your uncooked turkey
2 cups chicken broth, or as needed
1 loaf stale French bread, crumbled
2 cups crumbled cornbread
3 dozen shucked oysters, liqueur
   reserved
½ cup (1 stick) unsalted butter

1 large red onion, chopped
2 bunches green onions, chopped
8 garlic cloves, chopped fine
1 bunch celery, chopped
½ bunch parsley, chopped
1 (10½-ounce) can cream of
   mushroom soup

Place the turkey neck, gizzards, and heart in a medium pot, and pour in enough chicken stock to cover. Bring to a boil over high heat, and cook for 90 minutes. Reduce heat to medium-low and add the liver, then simmer for about 25 minutes longer. Remove the turkey giblets from the pan with a slotted spoon, and chop when cool enough to handle. Reserve the chicken broth.

Butter a 10 x 15-inch glass baking dish. In a medium bowl, cover the French bread and cornbread with the reserved oyster liqueur and chicken stock and set aside to soak. Melt the butter in a large skillet over medium heat. Add the chopped giblets and fry in the butter (because I said seaux). One at a time, add the red onion, green onions, garlic, celery, and parsley, cooking and stirring between each addition. Add the oysters and cream of mushroom soup to the pan. Stir to combine, and cook over medium heat for 12 minutes. Pour the mixture into a large bowl with the soaked bread. Transfer this mixture into the prepared baking dish. Bake for 45 minutes at 350°F until most of the water has evaporated, and then brown the top under the broiler if necessary.

→ Hallelujah Black-Eyed Peas and Ham Hocks

After you try this dish out you will definitely shout out, "Hallelujah, that's some good peas!"

Serves 8 to 10

1 pound dried black-eyed peas
3 cups water
2 smoked ham hocks
1 tablespoon Creole/Cajun spice

1 bay leaf
cooked white rice and cornbread, to serve

Soak the peas in water overnight. Drain and rinse them thoroughly, removing any tiny pebbles or other debris right before you are ready to cook them.

In a large stockpot over high heat, bring the water to a boil with the peas, ham hocks, spice, and bay leaf. Reduce the heat to medium-low and simmer, uncovered, 1½ hours, or until the peas are no longer crunchy and the ham hocks separate from the bone. Remove the bones from the ham hocks. Serve with white rice and cornbread.

→ Ernestine's Easy-Peasy Black-Eyed Peas and Rice

This not only makes a good side dish, but it is great by itself served over rice with freshly baked cornbread and collard or mustard greens. Trappey's brand black-eyed peas are great for this dish, if you can find them.

Serves 4 to 8

1 pound ground beef
3 cups Holy Trinity (page 16)
2 cups water

1 cup long-grain white rice
1 tablespoon Creole/Cajun spice
2 (15.5-ounce) cans black-eyed peas

In a 4-inch-high cast-iron skillet, fry the ground beef over medium-high heat. Add the Holy Trinity and sauté until the beef is brown. Drain the beef in a colander and add it back to the skillet. Add the water, rice, and the Creole/Cajun spice to the pan. Bring to a boil over high heat, cover, and reduce the heat to medium-low. Simmer for about 20 minutes, then add the peas and simmer for 20 minutes longer. Taste and adjust with more Creole/Cajun spice as needed.

⇢ Who Dat Potato Salad

This potato salad is not the typical picnic, Sunday church, or funeral version you are used to. It combines shrimp and the seasonings and spices of south Louisiana and will tempt you to eat it by the spoonful.

Serves 4

3 tablespoons peanut or canola oil
2 links andouille sausage, thinly sliced
14 small red potatoes, such as Red Bliss
1 pound medium uncooked shrimp, peeled and deveined
6 hard-cooked eggs, coarsely chopped

1 cup ranch dressing
2 tablespoons chopped parsley leaves
1 cup Holy Trinity Wit da Pope (page 16)
1½ tablespoons of Creole/Cajun spice

Heat the oil in a medium skillet over medium-high heat, and cook the sausage until it begins to brown, 5 to 10 minutes. Remove with a slotted spoon and set aside. Place the potatoes in a medium saucepan and add enough water to cover by 1 inch. Bring to a boil over high heat and cook for 15 minutes. Add the shrimp, cover, and cook until the shrimp turn pink and the potatoes are tender, about 5 minutes longer. Drain, refrigerate for about an hour, and then cut the potatoes into halves.

In a large bowl, combine the potatoes, sausage, shrimp, hard-cooked eggs, ranch dressing, parsley, Holy Trinity, and the Creole/Cajun spice. Toss gently until all ingredients are well mixed. Refrigerate the salad for several hours before serving to get it all good and married and not just living in sin.

Origins of the "Who Dat" Chant

"Who dat" is a phrase most commonly heard among New Orleans Saints fans to suggest that they can't be beat. However, the phrase has been around for over a century, appearing in poetry, song, film, and minstrel shows in the mid-twentieth century. Its origins as a sports chant are varied, with New Orleanians claiming that it originated at St. Augustine High School, a historically African-American all-boys parochial school founded in 1951. St. Aug was instrumental in the desegregation of high school athletics in Louisiana in the late 1960s, allowing its students to play against all-white schools.

Saints fans took up the chant and became the "Who Dat Nation," calling themselves "Who Dats." This originated from a song in the early 1980s by Aaron Neville that included several Saints players chanting, "Who Dat?, Who Dat?, Who Dat say dey gonna beat dem Saints?" in the chorus.

During Katrina, the Saints became a band of gypsies because of the devastating damage done by the flooding and hurricane. The Superdome was used as a shelter for NOLA residents who were not able to leave before the storm. Because of the renovations needed to the "Dome," the team was without a home for one season. As a result, they played in the San Antonio Alamo Dome and at LSU's Tiger Stadium in Baton Rouge. After the 2005 season Coach Sean Payton was hired as the head coach who then brought in Drew Brees, a player with the San Diego Chargers. Within three seasons, Coach Payton and Drew led the team to Super Bowl XLIV where they beat Payton Manning (a NOLA native and son of former Saint Archie) and the Indianapolis Colts 31–17, fueling the most exciting and raucous celebration the city has ever seen. Fans spread throughout the streets of the Tremé and French Quarter to chant "Who dat?, Who dat?, Who dat sey dey gonna beat dem Saints?!!!"

→ Isabella's Cracklin' Cornbread

This recipe is named for actress Isabella Rossellini, daughter of Ingrid Bergman, who first appears in HBO's *Tremé* as Annie Tee's mother in the third season.

Serves 8

1½ cups white cornmeal
½ cup all-purpose flour
1 tablespoon baking powder
¾ teaspoon baking soda
½ teaspoon salt
dash black pepper

1 cup Miss Gladiola's Big Easy
 Cracklins (page 58)
1 cup buttermilk
¼ cup vegetable oil or bacon
 drippings

Preheat the oven to 425°F. Stir together the cornmeal, flour, baking powder, baking soda, salt, pepper, and cracklins in a large bowl. Add the buttermilk and stir to combine well.

Heat the oil or bacon drippings in a 12-inch cast-iron skillet and heat over medium heat. Add the hot oil or bacon drippings to the batter, leaving 1 to 2 tablespoons in the skillet. Stir to combine well. Pour the mixture into the hot skillet, transfer the skillet to the oven, and bake until golden brown or a toothpick inserted in the center comes out clean, about 25 minutes.

⤳ Hushpeoples

This spicy recipe makes hushpuppies so hot they hush people, too! These are guaranteed to hush up any big mouth in the family, so serve them to your least favorite aunt or the in-law of your choice. Eat at your own risk! Hushpuppies are nothing more than a stiff, fried cornbread batter often served as an accompaniment to fried seafood. Note: Wash your hands thoroughly after handling the habañero peppers, some of the world's hottest peppers, and do not touch eyes or private parts (or any other sensitive places, for that matter) without first washing your hands with soapy water.

Serves 8 to 12

canola oil, for frying
1 cup all-purpose flour
1½ cups cornmeal
3 large eggs, beaten
1 bunch green onions, finely
  chopped
2½ cups warm milk

1 cup corn kernels
2 teaspoons baking powder
2 teaspoons chopped habañero
  pepper
1½ cups shredded American cheese
2 tablespoons melted unsalted
  butter

Pour about 3 inches of oil into a large cast-iron Dutch oven and heat to 350°F. Stir the flour and cornmeal together in a large bowl. Add the eggs to the flour mixture. Add the green onions, warm milk, corn, baking powder, and habañero pepper, and stir to combine well. Add the American cheese and the butter, and stir to thoroughly combine. When the oil is hot, drop the batter into the oil a spoonful at a time. Fry until your hushpeoples float and are golden brown in color. Drain on paper towels and serve hot.

→ Arthur's Shrimp 'n' Okra Hushpuppies

Stroll down any street of Tremé on a Sunday morning and the sounds of gospel music can be heard on almost any corner. You can be assured that the one of these joyful voices has plans to fry up some of these delicious pups for Sunday dinner.

Serves 8 to 12

 corn oil, for frying
1 cup self-rising yellow cornmeal
½ cup self-rising flour
1 cup medium uncooked shrimp,
    chopped
1 teaspoon Creole/Cajun spice
2 tablespoons finely diced onion
2 tablespoons finely diced green
    bell pepper

2 tablespoons finely diced celery
1 tablespoon minced garlic
½ cup frozen cut okra, thawed and
    chopped
1 large egg, lightly beaten
¾ cup lager beer

Pour the oil into a large Dutch oven to a depth of 4 inches, and heat to 350°F. In a large bowl, stir together the cornmeal and flour until mixed well. Sprinkle the shrimp with the Creole/Cajun spice. Add the shrimp, onions, bell peppers, celery, garlic, and okra to the cornmeal mixture and stir to combine. Stir in the egg and beer just until the cornmeal is moist. Let stand 7 minutes.

When the oil is hot, use a small ice cream scoop to drop the batter into the oil, and fry in batches until golden, about 2 minutes on each side. Drain on paper towels. Serve hot.

Mr. Okra

Mr. Okra, Arthur Robinson, is often referred to as "the last of the Creole vegetable vendors." In his colorful truck, he brings fresh, quality produce to the neighborhoods of New Orleans, and is a regular presence in the Tremé. His business is a remnant of times long ago when such vendors were common and filled Congo Square with their offerings, chanting their sing-song advertisements for items like fruits, vegetables, and calas. Some locals have described Mr. Okra's voice as a booming bullfrog baritone as he brags of his wares over the truck's loudspeaker. In the old days, other similar vendors had horse-drawn carts. Some of the more memorable ones included the ice man, the coffee man, the Roman candy man, and the charcoal man. My Maw-Maw once told me that when she was a girl, some of them even announced their arrival with the notes of a trumpet!

→ LaDonna's Crawfish Bread

This is a great lunchtime treat or appetizer for a party. You can make the topping in advance and then heat the bread up right before you are ready to serve. Just assemble, pop in the oven, and slice to finger food size. You'll be a big hit at your next event.

½ cup (1 stick) unsalted butter
2 cups Holy Trinity (page 16)
¼ cup water
1 cup chicken broth
⅓ cup Skillet Roux or Oven-Baked
   Roux (page 20)
½ teaspoon dried basil
1 (6-ounce) can Ro-Tel tomatoes
2 pounds Louisiana crawfish tails,
   with fat

1 (10½-ounce) can cream of shrimp
   soup
½ cup chopped green onions
½ cup chopped parsley
1 teaspoon Creole/Cajun spice
4 (6-inch) loaves French bread,
   halved lengthwise
1 pound shredded cheese, any kind
1 cup grated Parmesan cheese

In a large heavy pot or skillet, melt the butter and sauté the Holy Trinity until soft, about 5 minutes. Add the water and increase the heat to high until boiling. Add the chicken broth, dry roux, and basil. Return to a boil and then reduce the heat to medium and cook for 5 minutes.

Preheat the oven to 350°F. Add the tomatoes, crawfish tails, cream of shrimp soup, green onions, and parsley to the pot. Mix well and let simmer over medium heat until fairly thick, about 10 minutes.

Place the split loaves of French bread on a rimmed baking sheet and evenly spread the shredded cheese on top. Bake until the cheese melts, about 5 minutes. Evenly spread the crawfish mixture on the French bread. Spread the Parmesan on top and return to the oven under the broiler to brown, 2 to 3 minutes. Serve immediately.

➤ Po' Boys

"Bunny Bread and a thick slice of Creole tomato, salt, pepper, and an abundance of Blue Plate mayonnaise. Now, that's living!"

—*JOHN BESH*

A po' boy is a traditional submarine sandwich from Louisiana. It almost always consists of meat or seafood, usually fried, and it's served on an entire small loaf or about a quarter of a very long loaf, of baguettelike Louisiana French bread, sliced lengthwise into a top and bottom. Louisiana restaurants ask you if you want your po' boy "dressed," which means with mayonnaise, lettuce and tomatoes, or any other condiments you desire, often Creole mustard, ketchup, olive salad, or another dressing or sauce. Then you lay your meat and cheese along the length of the loaf, add pickles if you wish, and close it up and cut the loaf into shorter sandwiches suitable for everyone to share.

Some popular tasty combinations for cold po' boys include ham and roast beef and cold shrimp or crabmeat salad. Salami, bologna, pastrami, and corned beef are all excellent "stuffings," and two kinds of cheese are often added. Popular ingredients for hot po' boys are fried oysters, shrimp, crawfish, or catfish, and meatballs and tomato or barbecue sauce. In the last episode of the first season of the *Tremé* series, Davis McAlary says, "Po' boys aren't sandwiches; they're a way of life." This rings true to any New Orleanian, and there's a po' boy joint on almost any corner in the city. Some of the best are in Tremé.

Sandwiches for Strikers

The po' boy was invented during the turbulent strikes carried out by New Orleans streetcar motormen and conductors in the early 1930s. Martin Brothers Coffee Stand and Restaurant in the French Market was a popular eatery then. Its proprietors, Bennie and Clovis Martin, were former streetcar workers themselves and began feeding the striking workers for free. The name of the sandwich was coined "the poor boy" by Bennie, and was later shortened to po' boy.

→ Baby, I Knead You!
Homemade Po' Boy Bread

A true NOLA po' boy is all about the bread. Some natives say it's the water that makes NOLA French bread unique; some say it's the humidity down here. This recipe comes pretty close to the real deal. You can also go online and order up some authentic po' boy bread; try www.gambinos.com.

Makes enough for 4 sandwiches

4 cups all-purpose flour
1 cup cake flour
1 packet (2¼ teaspoons) active dry
  yeast
2 tablespoons nonfat dry milk

1 tablespoon sugar
1 tablespoon salt
2 cups hot water (130°F)
1 tablespoon unsalted butter
1 tablespoon cold water

In a stand mixer fitted with the paddle attachment, mix together 1 cup of the all-purpose flour and the cake flour, along with the yeast, dry milk, sugar, and salt. Pour in the hot water and butter, mix well, then add the remaining flour ½ cup at a time. When you're almost done adding the flour, switch to the dough hook attachment. Add more flour if needed to get an elastic but not sticky ball of dough. Cover the bowl with a clean kitchen towel and let rest for 12 minutes.

Knead on speed 2 for about 12 minutes. The dough should clean the sides of the bowl. Turn out into a lightly oiled bowl with a capacity at least 2½ times the size of the dough. Cover with a clean kitchen towel and let rise until doubled.

Punch down the dough and turn it out onto a lightly floured surface. Knead briefly, then divide into 2 pieces. Shape one half at a time into a loose rectangle. Cover loosely and let rest for 12 minutes.

Line a rimmed baking sheet with parchment paper. Press and roll each half of the dough into a 10 x 16-inch rectangle. Use your fingers to roll the dough into a 10-inch-long log. Seal the seam and ends. Roll and stretch each log to the length of the longest side of the parchment and place on the prepared baking sheet. Cover loosely with plastic wrap and let rise for 50 minutes. The dough should double easily.

Preheat the oven to 400°F. Brush the dough with cold water and use a sharp knife to cut slashes in the top of each log. Place an ovenproof dish on the lowest oven rack and fill the dish with hot water to create steam in the oven; this will help ensure that the crust on your bread is crispy while the inside stays tender. Bake the dough until golden brown, about 35 minutes, rotating the pan halfway through for even color. Cool on a wire rack.

→ Lt. Colson and Toni's Soft-Shell Crab Po' Boy Lunch

When these two meet at Casamento's (4330 Magazine Street) for lunch in an episode of *Tremé*, I would bet they have a dozen raw oysters on the half shell and then maybe, if in season, the soft-shell crab loaf.

Serves 1

peanut oil, for frying
1 large or 2 small soft-shell crabs
1 cup all-purpose flour
2 teaspoons salt
2 teaspoons black pepper
2 lettuce leaves

1 Creole tomato
2 tablespoons mayonnaise
½ teaspoon cayenne pepper
1 (8-inch loaf) po' boy bread (page 100) or French bread, to serve

Pour about 3 inches of peanut oil into a large, heavy pot and heat to 375°F. Thoroughly clean the soft-shell crabs (instructions follow).

In a medium bowl, stir together the flour, salt, and black pepper. When the oil is hot, powder the crabs with the flour mixture. Carefully add the crabs to the hot oil fry until they float and are golden brown, about 3 minutes. Do not overfry them. Remove from the oil with a slotted spoon, and drain the crabs on paper towels. If you want to cook more than 1 crab, I suggest you use the largest pot you can find and increase the oil. These critters take up a lot of oil and you need to make sure there is plenty of space in the oil and that the pot is not too crowded.

Assemble the po' boy with the crabs and the lettuce, tomato, mayonnaise, and cayenne pepper.

Cleaning Soft-Shell Crab

I've had some really foul-tasting soft-shells in my time, and it's usually because they weren't cleaned properly. This is a must or your crabs will taste very fishy.

- Thoroughly rinse the crab in cold tap water. Cut off the front of the crab with kitchen shears about ¼ to ½ inch behind the eyes.
- Turn the crab on its back and remove the apron-link shell.
- Pull back the top flap from the back and remove the crab's organs.
- Pull the right and left sides of the outer covering off the top of the crab and remove the gills.
- Thoroughly rinse the crab again, and cook or refrigerate immediately.

→ Sonny's Oyster Po' Boy

The character Sonny in the *Tremé* series has a serious drug addiction, and his fellow band member, bass player Cornell Williams, comes up with a plan to get him straight by putting him under the wings of a Vietnamese boat captain in lower Plaquemines parish. The scenes with Sonny on the boat give a true depiction of what it's like to be a shrimper, crabber, or oyster harvester in south Louisiana.

Serves 4

vegetable oil, for frying
3 large eggs
½ cup whole milk
1 quart shucked oysters, drained
3 cups cornmeal
¼ cup corn flour
1 tablespoon salt

1 tablespoon Creole/Cajun spice
1 teaspoon black pepper
4 (6-inch) loaves French bread
mayonnaise
shredded lettuce
2 medium tomatoes, sliced
dill pickle slices

Pour vegetable oil into a large, heavy cast-iron pot to a depth of 4 inches and heat to 350°F. While the oil is heating, in a medium bowl, beat the eggs and milk together. Add the oysters and let stand for 5 minutes.

Line a plate with paper towels. In a large bowl, stir together the cornmeal, flour, salt, Creole/Cajun spice, and pepper. Dip the oysters, 6 at a time, into the cornmeal and corn flour mixture. Carefully place in the hot oil at 350°F, and cook until the oysters float, about 3 minutes. Remove with a slotted spoon and drain on the paper towel–lined plate. Keep warm in a 200°F oven. Repeat with the remaining oysters.

Cut each loaf of bread three-quarters of the way through, leaving a hinge. Spread the mayonnaise on the inside of the bread. On the bottom half of the bread, arrange layers of shredded lettuce, fried oysters, tomato slices, and sliced pickles. Sprinkle with salt and pepper.

✦ Dr. John's Roast Beef Po' Boy with Debris Gravy

This classic po' boy is named for famed New Orleans jazz musician Dr. John, a classic himself. He is the winner of five Grammy awards and is a member of the Rock and Roll Hall of Fame. Dr. John made several cameo appearances as himself in HBO's *Tremé* series. Ask at your local butcher or deli for the end piece of roast beef used in his po' boy. To make this a Ferdi Special, à la Mother's Restaurant, the New Orleans spot famous for its ham, add good-quality sliced ham underneath the beef!

Makes 4

½ cup medium-brown Traditional Roux (page 104)
½ cup Holy Trinity (page 16)
2 cups beef stock (prepared or from bouillon), at room temperature
½ pound end piece of a roast beef, finely chopped
1 tablespoon Creole/Cajun spice

4 (6-inch) loaves Baby, I Knead You! Homemade Po' Boy Bread (page 100)
mayonnaise
Creole mustard
1 cup shredded cabbage
pickles
2 pounds high-quality sliced deli roast beef

Make the roux in a medium cast-iron pot. Over medium-high heat, sauté the Holy Trinity in the roux until the onions are tender, 5 to 7 minutes. Remove from the heat and let cool for 5 minutes. Slowly whisk in the beef stock and return to medium-high heat. Bring the gravy to a boil, reduce the heat to medium-low, and simmer for about 5 minutes, stirring frequently. Add the Creole/Cajun spice and the chopped roast beef end piece to the gravy and simmer another 5 minutes. The gravy should not be too thick. It should just coat the back of a wooden spoon. If you find it's too thick, add a bit more beef stock.

Assemble the sandwich by slicing the po' boy bread lengthwise leaving a hinge so that the bread stays together. Lay out the bread and add the mayonnaise, Creole mustard, a layer of cabbage, and the pickles. Mound ½ pound of the sliced roast beef on each sandwich, and ladle a generous amount of the gravy on top. Close it up and dig in. I suggest that you have a roll of paper towels on the table while eating this sandwich.

Mother's Restaurant

When you're in New Orleans, Mother's should be on your itinerary. They're located at 401 Poydras and are open from 7 a.m. to 10 p.m. seven days a week, every day of the year expect Thanksgiving, Christmas, Easter, and Mother's Day (of course). As their menu says, they do have the best baked ham that will ever tickle you taste buds, and Mother's is a New Orleans institution when it comes to the po' boy. They also have a great breakfast menu and serve many other traditional NOLA dishes.

Mother's didn't suffer extensive flood damage in Katrina, as many restaurants in the city did, so it didn't take long to reopen in the wake of the storm. The owners quickly found and gathered their faithful staff and set up FEMA trailers in the restaurant parking lot to house them. All went right to work getting the place back in pristine condition, and on October 15, 2005, they reopened with Vice Admiral Thad Allen, head of disaster relief, as their first customer. Along with the locals who flocked back to this New Orleans treasure, there was a whole new clientele from the disaster relief workers who were helping in the recovery effort. You'll find laborers, lawyers, tourists, and celebrities enjoying Mother's Roast Beef with Debris Gravy or the Ferdi Special with gravy dripping down to their elbows.

Ferdi Special at Mother's

→ North Roman Street Crawfish and Andouille Pizza on French Bread

This open-faced version of classic American pizza is perfect for feeding the neighborhood kids at birthday parties or for sleepovers. Next time, make it NOLA style and I bet they'll think you are great!

Serves 3 to 4

½ pound andouille sausage, diced
2 cups Holy Trinity Wit da Pope
   (page 16)
1 pound crawfish tails, without fat
1 tablespoon Creole/Cajun spice

1 (16-ounce) loaf French bread
1 (14-ounce) jar pizza or pasta
   sauce
3 cups shredded provolone cheese
   (about 12 ounces)

Preheat the oven to 425°F. Place a 12-inch skillet over medium heat. When the skillet is hot, add the sausage and cook until lightly browned on all sides, 4 to 5 minutes. Add the Holy Trinity Wit da Pope, increase the heat to medium-high, and sauté until the vegetables are tender, 5 to 7 minutes. Stir in the crawfish tails and the Creole/Cajun spice, and remove from the heat.

Cut the bread in half lengthwise. Cut each half crosswise into 3 equal pieces. Place the bread cut-side up on a baking sheet. Spread the pizza or pasta sauce evenly over the bread halves; top evenly with the crawfish mixture, and sprinkle with the provolone cheese. Bake until the cheese melts, about 13 minutes. Serve hot.

Zapp's Potato Chips

A favorite accompaniment to any po' boy is the tasty potato chips from south Louisiana made by Zapp's. These kettle chips are thicker than most and come in several flavors that have a Creole/Cajun flair, like Spicy Cajun Crawtators, Cajun Dill, Spicy Creole Tomato, Voodoo, Who Dat?, and LSU Tiger Tators. You can find these chips in grocers in the Southeast or online at www.zapps.com.

Muffulettas

The muffuletta is an Italian sandwich that originated around the French Market area of the French Quarter. It consists of a round flattened loaf of hearty, dense bread. The loaf is cut horizontally and layered with Italian cheeses and cold cuts. It can be served cold, or some restaurants warm it in the oven, which brings out the oils and flavors of the meat and cheese. An olive salad is then spread on the sandwich and then it's assembled. The traditional muffulettta is large enough to serve two to four people. The muffuletta originated at Central Grocery at 923 Decatur Street in the early 1900s. They still serve muffulettas just like they did for the Italian farmers who frequented the store back then. This is a must on your NOLA bucket list.

The Muffuletta Sandwich

This sandwich originated at Central Grocery, near NOLA's famous French Market, in the early 1900s. The story goes that, because of the grocery's proximity to the market, many of the Sicilian farmers who sold their goods there would visit Central Grocery for lunch. For a long time, the owner simply served typical Italian meats, cheese, and bread, but one day he created a sandwich out of all his regular ingredients and added muffuletta salad to them. It was an immediate hit with the farmers, and they came in and started ordering the "muffuletta."

Th
as
pl
Th

Entrées

Because of its proximity to the Gulf of Mexico, seafood is a major industry in Louisiana, and when natural or man-made disasters occur off the coast, one of the first concerns is the effect it will have on the creatures of the Gulf. After Hurricane Katrina in 2005, there were major setbacks to the seafood industry. Many folks who go out in their shrimp trawlers, fishing rigs, and oyster-harvesting boats lost their vessels and were devastated by the storm. However, it didn't take too long before they were back at their trade.

Things were looking up until the massive Deepwater Horizon oil spill in 2010, which caused such widespread pollution that many fisheries were effectively closed, and with them went the family fishing operations and small businesses. The spirit and resolve of the people of south Louisiana is one of survival, and hopefully, recovery is imminent, but it's good to pay attention to the environmental impacts that affect our favorite food sources. Ask direct questions about where the seafood you're purchasing was caught and the quality of the fishery.

Although it's famous for its seafood, New Orleans cuisine also features beef, poultry, and pork, and you'll find meat entrées, ranging from the simple to the elaborate, served up daily in the finest restaurants in Tremé and the rest of the city and region. Another tradition in New Orleans is street cooking. It's not unusual to see elaborate grilling rigs set up for cooking at events and festivals, filling the air with aromatic smoke and the sweet smells of meats cooking on the grill. New Orleans-style barbecue has its roots in the traditions of the Cajun cochon de lait (roasting a pig over an open fire) and in African American styles of smoking meats. Sauces are typically sweet with a blend of sweet and hot peppers that make for a spicy basting sauce.

# Seafood

My doctor told me to stop having intimate dinners for four
unless there are three other people.

—*ORSON WELLES*

Some or the freshest seafood can be found in south Louisiana. Did you know that one-third of the domestic seafood consumed in the United States comes from the waters of the Gulf of Mexico off the cost of Louisiana? The Louisiana Seafood Promotion and Marketing Board (www.louisianaseafood.com) lists interesting facts about just how much of the seafood in the U.S. comes from the state. For instance, more than 90 percent of the nation's crawfish come from Louisiana. About 70 percent of the oysters caught in the U.S. come from the Gulf Coast. One year's shrimp catch down here, strung in a single line, would wrap around the Superdome 94,839 times. That's a lot of shrimp!

Barbecue Shrimp: Louisiana Comfort Food

In Tremé and the entire greater New Orleans area, barbecue shrimp has been a favorite meal for decades. While it may be called barbecue shrimp by the locals, it actually has nothing to do with barbecue sauce or barbecuing as you may understand them. This is just another one of those peculiar regional things. In fact, NOLA barbecue sauce is a butter sauce (no surprise there, y'all!), both rich and flavorful—a blend of butter, garlic, liquid smoke, Worcestershire sauce, thyme, lemon juice, black pepper, and, of course, red Louisiana hot pepper sauce, combined with other savory herbs and spices.

Barbecue shrimp is legendary in south Louisiana and is always a hit at casual dinner parties because it's foolproof. Barbecue your shrimp, spread out newspaper for the tablecloth, and use lots of large napkins (since this is a hands-on experience!). Make sure you have plenty of hot steamed rice, for those who want it to soak up the sauce, and ice cold New Orleans beer, like an Abita Amber. Finish the meal with homemade bread pudding accompanied by Louisiana chicory coffee. Something sweet is the perfect ending for this delicious Tremé favorite!

⇥ Pride of the Parish Crabmeat au Gratin

This rich and filling dish is a staple in many Creole and Cajun restaurants across south Louisiana. You'll find it from Orleans to Calcasieu parishes in many variations and flavorings, but the very best are always made with a thick, rich béchamel sauce, quality lump crab, and a nice mild cheese. I call for cheddar here, but you can substitute your favorite cheese instead. This dish goes perfectly with a good chardonnay!

Serves 4 to 8

½ cup unsalted butter
1 cup finely chopped white onion
1 tablespoon minced garlic
½ cup diced yellow bell pepper
1 rib celery, finely chopped
2 tablespoons chopped green onion
½ cup all-purpose flour
1 (12-ounce) can evaporated milk
1 teaspoon salt

1 tablespoon minced fresh parsley
½ teaspoon cayenne pepper
½ teaspoon black pepper
2 egg yolks, slightly beaten
1 pound fresh or packaged lump crabmeat (remove all shell fragments)
1 pound cheddar cheese, shredded

Preheat the oven to 375°F. Butter a 1½-quart casserole dish. Melt the butter in a large skillet over medium heat. Add the onion, garlic, bell pepper, and celery, and cook, stirring, until the onion is translucent, about 7 minutes. Add the green onions and cook, stirring, until softened, about 4 minutes. Add the flour and stir until incorporated. Gradually add the evaporated milk, salt, parsley, cayenne pepper, and black pepper, stirring constantly. Cook until thickened, about 5 minutes. Remove from the heat.

Add about 1 teaspoon of the sautéed vegetables to the beaten eggs and stir vigorously. Add the egg mixture to the remaining vegetables in the skillet and stir vigorously with a wooden spoon until thoroughly incorporated. Return the skillet to the stove over low heat and cook until thickened, about 5 minutes. Remove from the heat and gradually fold in the crabmeat.

Pour the mixture into the prepared casserole dish. Top evenly with the cheddar cheese, and bake until golden and bubbly, about 22 minutes.

✣ Creighton's Tulane Stuffed Crabs

Stuffed crabs can be really tasty treats or just down-right awful, pasty lumps of bread stuffing. On the TV series *Tremé*, Creighton Bernette (John Goodman), an English professor at Tulane, would argue that you need to use quality lump crabmeat for this dish. Try not to make the stuffing a mushy mess when mixing the ingredients.

Makes 12

1 cup (2 sticks) unsalted butter, divided
1 large yellow onion, finely chopped
½ rib celery, finely chopped
1 bunch green onions, finely chopped
1 tablespoon finely chopped garlic
1 teaspoon salt
¼ teaspoon black pepper
4 tablespoons finely minced flat-leaf parsley
2 dashes Louisiana-style hot sauce, or as needed (Crystal Hot Sauce is a NOLA favorite)

2 cups homemade crab stock or shrimp stock
3 cups cubed stale French bread (about ½ loaf)
1 cup homemade French bread crumbs
1 pound fresh or packaged lump crabmeat (remove all shell fragments)
12 crab shells, washed thoroughly

Preheat the oven to 400°F. Melt ¾ cup (1½ sticks) of the butter in a large, heavy skillet over medium-high heat. When the butter is sizzling, add the onions and celery and cook, stirring, until the onions begin to brown, about 5 minutes. Add the green onions, garlic, salt, and pepper, and continue to cook, stirring, until the vegetables are tender. Add the parsley and cook for 1 minute. Season to taste with the hot sauce. Add the crab or shrimp stock, gently mix, then increase the heat to high and bring to a boil.

When the mixture is boiling, remove from the heat. Add the bread cubes and breadcrumbs, and mix thoroughly, then let the mixture cool. Transfer 2½ to 3 cups of the bread mixture to a large bowl, breaking it up with your hands. Carefully mix in the crabmeat and use your hands to combine with the bread mixture. Try not to break the lumps up too much

Arrange the crab shells on a rimmed baking sheet, and stuff each shell with a generous amount of the stuffing. Melt the remaining ¼ cup (½ stick) butter and drizzle over the crabs. Bake until the tops are a light brown, about 10 minutes.

⤳ Fleur de Lis Pan-Fried Catfish

The fleur de lis (which means "flower of lily" in French) is a major symbol of Louisiana. In the aftermath of Hurricane Katrina, it became a symbol of grassroots support for the recovery effort. And it has a special place in the hearts of many Louisianans, as it's the symbol for the New Orleans Saints.

Serves 2

1 cup cornmeal
2 teaspoons cayenne pepper
2 teaspoons sweet paprika
1 teaspoon onion powder
1 cup milk

⅓ cup corn oil
4 (4-ounce) catfish fillets
4 garlic cloves, minced
salt

In a medium bowl, stir together cornmeal, cayenne pepper, paprika, and onion powder to combine well. Pour the mixture onto a large sheet of waxed paper. Pour the milk into a medium bowl.

Heat the corn oil in a large skillet over medium heat. Dip the catfish fillets into the milk and hold up to let the milk drip off. Roll the milk-soaked fillets in the cornmeal mixture until completely covered. Set aside.

When the oil is hot, briefly fry the garlic in the skillet; do not let the garlic burn. Add the coated catfish fillets to the skillet and cook until golden on one side, about 6 minutes. Turn the fillets over, sprinkle with salt, and cook on the second side until golden and the fish flakes easily with a fork, about 6 minutes longer. Drain on paper towels. Serve with French fries, hushpuppies, and cold slaw.

Louisiana Seafood Safety

Many folks have expressed concern and there have been several negative reports in the media as to the safety of Gulf Coast seafood after the Deepwater Horizon oil spill of 2010. It should be pointed out that the Louisiana seafood industry is the most regulated in the United States. According to the Louisiana Department of Wildlife and Fisheries, it has been found that the average person could consume 63 pounds of shrimp (1575 jumbos), 5 pounds of oyster meat (130 on the half shell), and 9 pounds of fish (eighteen 8-ounce filets) each day for up to five years without exceeding health risks for contamination of the chemicals used to clean up the spill. Not even the most ardent south Louisianan could eat this much seafood! So enjoy and don't worry too much about what you hear.

→ North Rampart Street
Creole Tomato Jambalaya

North Rampart is the southern boundary between Tremé and the French Quarter. It was known as the central district for African-American culture and commerce in the early- and mid-twentieth century. Along this four-lane street with a tree-lined median, you'll find Louis Armstrong Park, Our Lady of Guadalupe Chapel, the Eagle Saloon and Oddfellows Hall, the Saenger Theater, and the J&M Music Store where many classic jazz tunes were recorded.

Serves 4

2 tablespoons unsalted butter
2 cups Holy Trinity Wit da Pope
  (page 16)
2 pounds Creole Tasso (page 17)
2 large Creole tomatoes, diced
1 (10.5-ounce) can condensed beef
  broth, undiluted
1 cup long-grain white rice

1 cup water
1 teaspoon sugar
1 teaspoon dried thyme
1 tablespoon Creole/Cajun spice
1½ pounds uncooked medium to
  large shrimp, peeled and deveined
1 tablespoon minced fresh parsley

Melt the butter in a 6 to 8-quart Dutch oven over medium heat. Add the Holy Trinity Wit da Pope, and cook, stirring, until tender, about 7 minutes. Stir in the tasso, tomatoes, beef broth, rice, water, sugar, thyme, Creole/Cajun spice, and bring to a boil over high heat. Reduce the heat to medium-low, cover, and simmer until the rice is tender, about 25 minutes. Add the shrimp and parsley, and simmer, uncovered, until the shrimp turn pink, 7 to 10 minutes. Serve hot.

Creole Jambalaya

Creole jambalaya originated in the French quarter, where the Spanish created a new version of the saffron-spiced paella because saffron was not readily available locally. Later French and Caribbean influences helped create the dish's now-famous spices and flavor. The Creole version uses tomatoes (the Cajun counterpart doesn't). Cajun jambalayas, which are smokier and spicier than the Creole variety, originated from the swamps of south Louisiana and are usually brown in color.

↘ Delmond's Creole Tomato Festival Shrimp

This legendary dish is a tomato-based Creole sauce that's usually served over rice and normally includes fresh Gulf Coast shrimp, although other seafood may be substituted. It differs from gumbo because it is not based on a roux and is often spicier and thicker. This recipe is named after Delmond on the *Tremé* series because he struggles with his Creole/New Orleans heritage, but eventually comes around to appreciate his background and the traditions of his father, Albert "Big Chief" Lambreaux.

Serves 4

1 tablespoon olive oil
1 large onion, diced
1 large green bell pepper, diced
4 ribs celery, chopped
2 garlic cloves, minced
1½ pounds medium shrimp, peeled
   and deveined
2 medium, fresh Creole tomatoes,
   finely diced

1 (10-ounce) can diced tomatoes
   with green chilies
1 (6-ounce) can tomato paste
¾ cup chicken broth
1 teaspoon crushed red pepper
1 teaspoon onion powder
1 teaspoon garlic powder
2 teaspoons salt
2 teaspoons black pepper
hot cooked white rice, to serve

Heat the olive oil in large skillet over medium heat. Add the onion, bell pepper, and celery, and cook, stirring, until tender, about 5 minutes. Add garlic and cook 1 to 2 minutes longer.

Add the shrimp, tomatoes, green chilies, and stir well. Reduce the heat to medium-low so the mixture is simmering. In a medium bowl, stir the tomato paste into the chicken broth, mix well, and add to the pan. Add the crushed red pepper, onion powder, garlic powder, salt, and black pepper, and cook, stirring often, until the shrimp are firm and the sauce begins to thicken, about 15 minutes. Serve over rice.

⤜ It's Your Birthday Creamy Crawfish Pastalaya

Although there is no known origin for this variation on the traditional jambalaya, some believe that this dish came to be because of the growing popularity of pasta dishes in recent years. Using pasta intstead of rice was a natural transition from a typically Spanish-influenced dish to one with an Italian twist.

Serves 4

½ pound smoked andouille sausage
2 tablespoons extra-virgin olive oil
2 cups Holy Trinity Wit da Pope
  (page 16)
3 green onions, chopped, white and
  green parts divided
1 teaspoon Italian seasoning blend
2 cups heavy cream
½ pound linguine, fettuccine, or
  other pasta (penne works well)

1 pound Louisiana crawfish tails,
  with fat (do not drain)
2 tablespoons chopped flat-leaf
  parsley
½ cup grated good-quality
  Parmesan, plus more to serve
Creole/Cajun spice

Heat a large, heavy saucepan over medium-high heat. Slice the sausage into ¼-inch circles, and place in the hot pan to brown on both sides. Add the olive oil, the Holy Trinity, and the white parts of the green onions, and cook, stirring, until soft, about 5 minutes. Add the Italian seasoning, and season to taste with the Creole/Cajun spice. Stir in the cream and reduce the heat to medium-low. Cook until thickened, about 8 minutes.

Meanwhile, cook the pasta according to package directions, just to al dente. Drain, toss with a little olive oil or a bit of the cream sauce to avoid starchiness, and keep it warm in the covered pot.

Add the crawfish to the cream mixture and simmer for 5 minutes. Add the green parts of the green onions and the parsley, and simmer 1 minute longer. Remove from the heat and stir in the Parmesan cheese.

When ready to serve, toss the crawfish cream sauce with the pasta and serve on large platter. At the table, offer extra Parmesan to sprinkle on top, if desired.

⤳ Everette's New Orleans–Style Barbecued Shrimp

Barbecued shrimp was big news when it was developed back in the 1950s at Pascal's Manale Restaurant on Napoleon Avenue just north of the Uptown neighborhood southeast of Tremé.

Serves 8 to 12

 4 pounds colossal shrimp, unpeeled and head on
½ pound unsalted butter, at room temperature
1 cup olive oil
4 teaspoons cayenne pepper
2 teaspoons salt
2 teaspoons ground thyme
4 teaspoons black pepper
1 teaspoon ground oregano
1 teaspoon ground basil
2 teaspoons smoked paprika
6 teaspoons crushed garlic

2 teaspoons ground rosemary
4 teaspoons Worcestershire sauce
2 teaspoons Louisiana-style hot sauce
2 teaspoons liquid smoke
1 teaspoon freshly squeezed lemon juice
3 bay leaves, finely crushed
½ cup fresh chopped parsley
1 (12-ounce) can lager beer
½ pound cold unsalted butter
French baguettes, to serve

Rinse and drain the shrimp. Spread in a shallow baking dish.

Combine ½ pound of the butter and all the ingredients except the baguettes and beer, in a medium saucepan over low heat and cook until the butter is melted. Let the mixture cool and pour it over the shrimp making sure they are fully immersed in the marinade. Cover, refrigerate, and marinate for several hours or overnight for best results, turning and basting several times.

Heat a large sauté pan over medium-high heat and add enough of the marinade to cover the bottom of the pan. Place enough shrimp (heads on and not peeled) from the marinade in the bottom of the pan and sauté until the shrimp turn pink, 3 to 5 minutes. Repeat this until you have cooked all of the shrimp. Place cooked shrimp in a serving dish. When all of the shrimp are cooked, remove the pan from the heat, add about 6 ounces of beer (then drink the rest) and the cold butter, and stir until the butter melts to make a sauce. Pour the sauce over the cooked shrimp in the serving dish. Serve in deep bowls with crusty French baguettes to soak up the yummy sauce. Serve with ice cold Abita Purple Haze.

→ Road Home Shrimp and Grits

On *Tremé*, while Jannette is at the end of her hiatus from NOLA in New York City, she prepares this dish while working under the tutelage of David Chang, a renowned New York chef. The dishes she prepares in these episodes are actually Chang's creations featured in his real-world restaurants.

3 cups water
¼ teaspoon salt
¾ cup grits
1 tablespoon peanut oil
1 small red bell pepper, chopped
1 tabasco pepper, seeded and chopped
1 small yellow onion, chopped
1 teaspoon minced garlic

1 pound large shrimp, peeled and deveined
1 tablespoon Suck da Heads and Pinch da Tails Creole Spice (page 13)
4 plum tomatoes, coarsely chopped
½ cup shredded mild cheddar cheese (about 4 ounces)

Bring the water and salt to a boil in a medium saucepan over high heat. Whisk in the grits, cover, and reduce the heat to low so the mixture is simmering. Cook, stirring occasionally, until smooth and thickened, 30 to 45 minutes.

Meanwhile, heat the oil in a large skillet over medium-high heat. Add the bell pepper, tabasco pepper, onion, and garlic, and cook, stirring, until soft, about 5 minutes. Add the shrimp and spice, stir, and cook for 2 minutes. Add the tomatoes and cook until the shrimp are pink, about 3 minutes, stirring frequently.

Remove the grits from the heat and stir in the cheddar cheese. Serve the shrimp and vegetables over the grits.

Grits and the South

You'll find grits on the menu at any breakfast joint south of the Mason–Dixon, and they often come without you ordering them. Grits have their origin in Native American preparation of coarsely ground corn. They can be either white or yellow and come in all flavors and textures. A true grits connoisseur will scold you if you suggest that they use instant grits or what are commonly called "quick grits." These varieties just don't have the texture or flavor of the ones you have to boil for a while.

Shrimp and grits are prepared all over the south, but I'll argue that some of the best can be found in Louisiana. Adding peppers and Creole spice can jazz up this dish.

☀ North Prieur Street Shrimp, Okra, and Tomato Sauté

Contrary to popular belief, okra doesn't have to be a slimy boiled mess. In this dish okra blends with the tomatoes to produce a wonderfully delicious stew. Okra was probably introduced to New Orleans through African and Caribbean slaves. This dish is delicious served with couscous and a crisp French baguette.

Serves 4

2 pounds uncooked jumbo shrimp, peeled and deveined
2 tablespoons Creole/Cajun spice, divided
8 ounces cubed Creole Tasso (page 17)
2 tablespoons peanut oil

3 tablespoons all-purpose flour
2 cups sliced fresh okra
1 pint grape tomatoes
1 cup fish stock (prepared or from boullion)
¼ teaspoon ground allspice
2 shallots, chopped

Season the shrimp with 1 tablespoon of the Creole/Cajun spice and set aside. In a large sauté pan over medium-high heat, brown the tasso in the peanut oil. Remove the tasso and set aside. Add the flour to the oil and whisk to make a chocolate-brown roux (see page 20). When the roux is done, add the okra and tomatoes and the remaining 1 tablespoon Creole/Cajun spice and sauté for about 2 minutes. Add the fish stock and allspice, mix well, and bring to a boil over medium-high heat. Lower the heat to medium and cook for 5 minutes longer, stirring frequently.

Add the shrimp and cook, stirring, until the shrimp turns pink, about 5 minutes. Mix in the green onions and the tasso. Cook another 2 minutes. Serve hot.

→ Shrimp Woodrow

I named this one after my paw-paw Woodrow. He loved to cook and was known for his jambalaya, but he could make just about anything.

Serves 4

- 2 pounds large shrimp, peeled and deveined
- ¾ cup olive oil
- 1 teaspoon salt
- 1 teaspoon freshly ground black pepper
- 1 teaspoon dried oregano
- 1 teaspoon dried rosemary
- 3 bay leaves
- 6 to 10 garlic cloves, unpeeled, mashed
- ½ cup dry white wine
- sliced French bread with garlic and butter, to serve

In a large skillet, over medium-high heat, combine the shrimp, olive oil, salt, pepper, oregano, rosemary, bay leaves, and garlic. Cook, stirring occasionally, until the shrimp are pink and the liquid produced by the shrimp has almost completely disappeared, 15 to 20 minutes. Reduce the heat to low, and add the wine. Cook at a low simmer until the liquid is reduced by half, 5 to 7 minutes. Serve the shrimp hot with the pan juices in individual serving dishes with crispy sliced French bread toast with garlic and butter.

Louisiana Fishermen

Asian fishing communities have been prominent along the Louisiana Gulf Coast since the end of the Vietnam War. Persecuted Catholics in Vietnam were encouraged to immigrate to Southern Louisiana by Bishop Dominic Luong, Hanoi native. Today more than 30 percent of all commercial seafood fishing in Louisiana is by Vietnamese Americans. There's also a large Vietnamese population in New Orleans, and their South Asian cuisine is popular among many residents of the city, as is the fusion of Vietnamese and Southern cuisine.

→ Mahalia's Abundantly Blessed Shrimp Spaghetti

It is a common practice in Tremé kitchens to make spaghetti sauce with shrimp or chicken. I guess this is because not everyone could afford beef in the old days, and fowl and seafood were plentiful and affordable to most residents.

Serves 4

1 (8-ounce) package spaghetti
2 tablespoons cornstarch
½ cup water
1 (14.5-ounce) can chicken broth
3 tablespoons canola oil
4 garlic cloves, minced
½ cup chopped red onion
⅛ teaspoon cayenne pepper

1½ pounds cooked medium to large
   shrimp, peeled and deveined
2 tablespoons freshly squeezed
   lemon juice
¼ teaspoon grated lemon zest
¼ cup minced fresh parsley
grated Parmesan cheese, to serve

Cook the spaghetti according to the package directions until al dente. Meanwhile, in a medium bowl, stir together the cornstarch, water, and chicken broth until smooth, and set aside. Heat the canola oil in a large skillet over medium-high heat, and cook the garlic, onion, and cayenne, stirring occasionally, until tender, about 5 minutes. Stir the broth mixture and add to the skillet. Bring to a boil over high heat, cook, and stir until thickened, about 2 minutes. Reduce the heat to medium, and add the shrimp, lemon juice, lemon zest, and parsley. Cook until heated through, 2 to 4 minutes.

When the spaghetti is cooked, drain and place it in a large bowl. Add the shrimp mixture and toss to coat. Serve hot with grated Parmesan cheese.

Mahalia Jackson

Laissez les bon temps roulez ("let the good times roll") in the Tremé at the Mahalia Jackson Theater at 801 North Rampart Street. Known around the globe as the "Queen of Gospel," Jackson, born and raised in New Orleans, was a civil rights activist who sang a memorable slave spiritual before Dr. Martin Luther King Jr. delivered the famous "I Have a Dream" speech in 1963. Home to the opera, symphony, and ballet, the theater also hosts a Broadway series and frequent popular music concerts.

→ Marigny Crawfish Étouffée

The Marigny (or Faubourg Marigny) is a neighborhood that borders the French Quarter on the northeast and is very close to Tremé. Hurricane Katrina was less severe on the Marigny than other parts of New Orleans. Étouffée (ay-TOO-fay), from the French word for "stuffed," refers to a Louisiana seafood-and-rice dish that is not actually stuffed but instead is "smothered" with a highly spiced sauce. It is a classic dish in New Orleans and is delicious made with shrimp or crawfish.

Serves 2 to 4

½ cup (1 stick) butter
2 tablespoons all-purpose flour
1 cup Holy Trinity Wit da Pope (page 16)
1 pound crawfish tails, with fat (do not rinse)
2 teaspoons tomato paste
1½ cups water

1 to 2 tablespoons Creole/Cajun spice
¼ cup chopped green onions, white parts only
¼ cup finely chopped fresh parsley
hot cooked long-grain white rice, to serve

Melt the butter in a large saucepan over medium heat. Make a roux, whisking the flour vigorously until light brown. Add the Holy Trinity Wit da Pope to the roux and sauté until tender, about 5 minutes. Reduce the heat to low, add the crawfish fat, and simmer for about 15 minutes. Add the crawfish tails and tomato paste, then add the water, mixing until smooth. Cook until reduced, about 20 minutes. Season to taste with Creole/Cajun spice. Cook about 10 minutes more. Add the green onions and parsley, and cook 5 minutes longer. Serve over rice.

→ Clotile's Crawfish and Brussels Sprouts

Clotile is the wife of the New Orleans Zephyrs AAA minor league baseball team mascot, a human-sized nutria rat named Boudreaux D. Nutria. These semi-aquatic rodents, related to the beaver family, feed on plants and sometimes small crustaceans such as crawfish. I bet they would love this dish. You will also sometimes hear these names in popular humorous Cajun stories and jokes about the infamous Boudreaux and Thibodeaux. Feel free to replace the crawfish tails in this recipe with 1 pound of shrimp.

Serves 2 to 4

1 pound small to medium Brussels
    sprouts
2 tablespoons light olive oil
1 small red onion, chopped
1 rib celery, chopped
2 garlic cloves, minced

2 tablespoons Creole/Cajun spice
1 pound crawfish tails, with fat
¾ cup dry white wine
1 cup chicken stock
¼ cup (½ stick) unsalted butter

Bring a medium pot of salted water to a boil. To prep the Brussels sprouts, first cut off the bottom end and peel off the first layer of leaves. Cook the Brussels sprouts in the boiling water until you are able to pierce the bottom of a sprout with a small knife with little resistance, about 4 minutes.

Heat a medium skillet over medium-high heat until hot and then add the olive oil. Add the onion, celery, garlic, Brussels sprouts, and Creole/Cajun spice, and cook, stirring or tossing occasionally, until slightly limp, 2 to 3 minutes. Add the crawfish tails. Deglaze the pan by adding the wine and stirring to loosen any brown bits on the bottom. Add the chicken stock and bring to a simmer. Cook until the stock is almost all evaporated. Add the butter, and serve when the butter is melted.

→ Harley's Crawfish Fettuccine

Harley, played by musician Steve Earle, provides some of the most memorable musical moments in the *Tremé* series. His song "This City," a tribute to post-Katrina New Orleans, is as rich as this dish is in its portrayal of the spirit of NOLA.

6 tablespoons unsalted butter
2½ cups Holy Trinity Wit da Pope
   (page 16)
1 tablespoon all-purpose flour
1 pound Louisiana crawfish tails
   with fat
1 (8-ounce) package Velveeta cheese

½ cup half-and-half
½ cup heavy cream
2 teaspoons Creole/Cajun spice
2 teaspoons cayenne pepper
1 pound fettuccine
½ cup grated Parmesan cheese

Melt the butter in a large skillet over medium heat. Cook the Holy Trinity, stirring, until the onions are tender, about 7 minutes. Stir in the flour, and cook, stirring frequently, about 8 minutes. Reduce the heat to low, cover, and simmer for 20 minutes, stirring often. Stir in the crawfish tails, Velveeta cheese, half-and-half, cream, Creole/Cajun spice, and cayenne pepper. Cover, and simmer for about 20 minutes, stirring occasionally.

Meanwhile, preheat the oven to 350°F, and butter a 9 x 13-inch baking dish. Bring a large pot of lightly salted water to a boil. Cook the fettuccine according to the package directions until al dente, about 10 minutes. Drain.

Stir the pasta into the crawfish mixture. Pour into the prepared dish and sprinkle with the Parmesan cheese. Bake until hot and bubbly, about 20 minutes.

→ Lizardi Street Crawfish Monica

This one is a must when you travel down to New Orleans for Jazz Fest in the spring. You've usually got to stand in line for a while to get this treat, as it's so popular, but it's worth it. This recipe will hold you over until you get down for the fest.

Serves 4 to 6

1 pound rainbow rotini pasta
½ cup (1 stick) unsalted butter
3 medium garlic cloves, finely minced
3 green onions, sliced

1 tablespoon of Creole/Cajun spice
1 pound Louisiana crawfish tails, with fat (do not rinse)
2 cups heavy cream
sliced toasted French bread, to serve

Cook the pasta according to the package directions until al dente. Rinse and drain.

Sauté the butter and garlic in a medium saucepan over medium heat for 2 minutes, then add the green onions and continue cooking for about 1 minute. Sprinkle in the Creole/Cajun spice and incorporate the crawfish tails with the fat. Simmer for about 2 minutes. Whisk in the heavy cream, reduce the heat to medium, and simmer until the sauce reduces by about half. Add the sauce to the pasta, stir to combine, and simmer over low heat for 5 minutes. Serve in shallow bowls over toasted slices of French bread.

International Shrine of St. Jude

Down in the Tremé, you'll want to check out the International Shrine of St. Jude, inside Our Lady of Guadalupe Church at 411 North Rampart Street. Built in 1826 by two French architects for $14,000, it's the oldest church building in the entire New Orleans metropolitan area. Originally a burial church for yellow fever victims, it is currently the official chapel for the New Orleans police and fire departments and is a lovely specimen among the many beautiful buildings in this magical neighborhood.

Chicken

Erotica is using a feather, pornography is using the whole chicken.

— *ISABEL ALLENDE*

Chickens in New Orleans have a long and interesting legacy. It was not uncommon before Katrina for local residents to have a chicken coop in their backyard for eggs and meat. After the flood, many of these birds escaped their captivity. Now, wild chickens roam the streets of the city and have become a nuisance to some and endeared cohabitants to others. Many homesteaders in post-Katrina New Orleans have restarted the practice of raising the birds as a cheap alternative to buying them at the grocer.

The Cajuns use chickens as important ingredients in many of their dishes as they are plentiful, easy to raise, and don't cost much to maintain. Chickens in the African-American community have been a staple in cooking since the early days of slavery.

An Asian Take on NOLA Chicken and Waffles

In a season 2 episode of *Tremé*, "That's What Lovers Do," Janette Dasautel cooks chicken and waffles for the restaurant crew after hours while she is working at the Lucky Peach, a fictionalized hybrid of New York chef David Chang's real-life restaurants Momofuku Ko and Momofuku Ssäm Bar. Her Asian take on this traditional Tremé neighborhood dish—white rice flour waffles and a spicy ginger vinaigrette reduction—was a big hit with the crew and chef, resulting in Chang offering Jannette a chance to feature her New Orleans dishes one night a week at the restaurant. For a more traditional take on chicken and waffles, check out my recipe on page 136.

⤳ Kaki's Cajun Lemon Stir-Fry

Being the melting pot that NOLA is, it's not surprising that Asian food has infused the city's cuisine. Melding the traditions of Asian cooking with those of New Orleans has resulted in totally new dining experiences. Don't hesitate to try out some of the local Asian offerings while visiting.

Serves 4

2 tablespoons peanut oil
1¼ pounds chicken tenders, cut in
   1-inch pieces
8 small sweet peppers, diced (mix of
   yellow, red, and orange)
½ large red onion, diced
1 tablespoon minced garlic

1½ tablespoons Creole/Cajun spice
¼ cup freshly squeezed lemon juice
¾ cup water
¼ cup sugar
2 tablespoons unsalted butter
2 tablespoons cornstarch
warm cooked rice, to serve

Heat the peanut oil in a large wok over medium-high heat. Add the chicken and cook, stirring occasionally, until almost cooked through, about 10 minutes. Add the peppers, onion, and garlic and sprinkle with the Creole/Cajun spice. Cook, stirring frequently, until the chicken is cooked through and the veggies are tender, about 5 minutes.

Meanwhile, in a small pan over medium-high heat, bring the lemon juice, water, and sugar to a boil. Boil until the sugar dissolves. Reduce the heat to medium, add the butter, and stir until melted. Stir in the cornstarch and simmer over low heat for about 3 minutes.

Pour the lemon sauce over the chicken and vegetables, stir, and heat for 2 minutes longer. The sauce will pick up some of the seasoning. Serve over warm rice.

Jazz Fest

The New Orleans Jazz and Heritage Festival, better known to locals as Jazz Fest, is the second-most popular draw to New Orleans every year behind Mardi Gras. Jazz Fest is a celebration of the culture and music of the Crescent City, not to mention an enticing assault on the senses with the smells and tastes of some of NOLA's most exciting cuisines and libations. The music is as diverse as the city itself, with appearances from many pop, rock, jazz, gospel, hip-hop, and folk musicians, often big-name performers. Such artists as Bruce Springsteen, the Eagles, the Foo Fighters, Jimmy Buffet, the Neville Brothers, Trombone Shorty, Herbie Hancock, Irma Thomas, Bonnie Raitt, Pete Fountain, and Asleep at the Wheel, and most major Cajun, zydeco, blues, and jazz artists from Louisiana have performed.

Roger Lewis, Tremé Brass Band

The inaugural festival in 1970 was held in Louis Armstrong Park, close to the original Congo Park in the Tremé. It grew so popular so fast that, two years later, the festival was moved to the New Orleans Fairgrounds and Racetrack and has been there ever since. The festival grounds are separated into twelve music venues of stages and tents with two enormous food areas where you can sample anything from the infamous icy treat unique to New Orleans, the sno-ball, to delectable Cajun and Creole delicacies, such as fried alligator and seafood gumbo.

If Mardi Gras isn't your thing, then try Jazz Fest. It's held the last weekend of April and the first weekend of May, and the weather is usually nice and comfortable compared with the sweltering heat of the summer, which is only for true summer-season aficionados.

Lloyd Meadows

→ Avondale Chicken Fricassee

"Fricassee" often describes stewed food, and the food in Tremé is known for bringing ingredients to the pot and simmering them until the meats are tender and have absorbed all of the flavors of the vegetables, herbs, and meats. This recipe does just that and produces a hearty, delicious meal for your hungry family.

Serves 4 to 8

¾ cup light olive oil
3 tablespoons all-purpose flour
1 tablespoon Creole/Cajun spice
1 (3-pound) chicken, cut into 8 pieces
1 cup Holy Trinity Wit da Pope (page 16)

1 teaspoon dried rosemary
1 teaspoon dried oregano
1 cup dry white wine
8 ounces sliced baby portabella mushrooms

Heat the oil in a large skillet over medium-high heat. In a small bowl, combine the flour and Creole/Cajun spice, and coat the chicken with the flour mixture. When the oil is hot, add the chicken pieces and cook, turning often, until browned. Add the Holy Trinity Wit da Pope, rosemary, and oregano to the pot, then stir to distribute evenly with the chicken. Pour in the wine and add the mushrooms, then simmer until the wine is reduced by half. Serve hot with the pan juices as a sauce.

→ Rebirth Kickin' Chicken and Wicked-Ass Waffles

This is the comfort food of all comfort foods, and has long been served in Tremé home kitchens. The of combination salty chicken, sweet waffles, and syrup makes your taste buds do a dance. For the most authentic NOLA flavor, serve your chicken and waffles with Steen's 100% Pure Cane Syrup.

Serves 4 to 8

1 cup salt
1 gallon (16 cups) water
1 (3½-pound) fryer chicken, cut
   into 8 pieces
peanut oil, for frying
4 cups all-purpose flour, divided
2 tablespoons Creole/Cajun spice
3½ teaspoons baking powder

1 teaspoon sugar
¼ teaspoon salt
2 large eggs
4 tablespoons unsalted butter,
   melted
1½ cups buttermilk
unsalted butter, to serve
pure cane syrup, to serve

Combine the salt and water in a large bowl to make a brine, and soak the chicken in the brine for about 30 minutes. Pour peanut oil into a deep, large cast-iron skillet or pot to a depth of about 3 inches. Heat the oil to 360°F over high heat. Reduce the heat to medium-high to maintain the temperature. Rinse the chicken pieces in cold water and leave them wet.

Place a wire rack over a rimmed baking sheet. In a large paper bag, combine 2 cups of the flour and the Creole/Cajun spice. Add the chicken pieces, fold the bag over to seal, and shake it good (like your happy ass at Mardi Gras). Remove the chicken from the bag and place on the wire rack. Let sit for about 12 minutes.

When the oil is hot, carefully add the chicken and fry, turning once, until golden brown, about 20 minutes total. Remove and drain on the wire rack.

Preheat the waffle iron. In a large bowl, sift together the remaining 2 cups flour and the baking powder, sugar, and salt. Beat the eggs in a medium bowl. Add the butter and buttermilk and beat to combine. Add the wet ingredients to the dry ingredients, and mix 'em up well with a wooden spoon! Spray the waffle iron with a cooking spray and pour the batter into the hot iron. Cook until golden brown. Repeat with the remaining batter.

To serve, top the waffles with a slice of butter, and serve with the frickin' kickin' chicken and 100% pure cane syrup. Heat the syrup before you pour it over the waffles and also drizzle a bit on the chicken. Yeah, you right!

→ Uncle Rain's Gospel Chicken

Some of the best fried bird in the world comes out of the grease right here in the Big Easy. This recipe uses thigh and leg meat, which has more flavor than the breast. And you got to have the skin on for that crispy crust so synonymous with Southern fried chicken. Geaux forth and munch-ify, y'all!

Serves 4 to 6

BRINING MIX
1 quart (4 cups) root beer
1 teaspoon liquid smoke
3 tablespoons Worcestershire sauce
1 tablespoon Louisiana-style hot sauce
3 garlic cloves, crushed
3 tablespoons coarse salt
2½ tablespoons black pepper

FRIED CHICKEN
¾ cup peanut oil, plus more for frying
lard, for frying
6 skin-on, bone-in chicken thighs
6 skin-on, bone-in chicken legs
1 large egg
2½ cups water
2 teaspoons baking powder
2 tablespoons Creole/Cajun spice
3 cups all-purpose flour
salt and black pepper

TO MAKE THE BRINING MIX: In a food processor or blender, purée the root beer, liquid smoke, Worcestershire sauce, hot sauce, garlic, salt, and pepper together well. Place the chicken in a large bowl and pour the brining mix on top. Cover and marinate for 5 hours in the refrigerator.

TO MAKE THE FRIED CHICKEN: Fill a large cast-iron skillet halfway with equal amounts peanut oil and lard. Slowly bring the temperature up to 375°F. While the oil is heating, remove the chicken from the brine and place in a colander, rinse in cold water, and drain.

In a large bowl, whisk the egg well, then whisk in the peanut oil and the water. In a medium bowl, stir together the baking powder, Creole/Cajun spice, and flour. Add the dry ingredients to the wet ingredients and whisk slowly until you have a smooth batter.

Pat the drained chicken dry with paper towels and season with salt and black pepper. When the oil is hot, dip the chicken in the batter and carefully place in the hot oil. Cook, turning regularly, until the chicken pieces float, 10 to 11 minutes. Remove a piece and prick it with a fork. It's done if the juices run clear. Drain on a wire rack, then transfer to paper towels to drain completely. If not, then continue frying for a few more minutes and test again. If the crust is getting too brown, you can also remove the chicken, transfer it to a baking sheet, lay a piece of foil on top, and bake it at 350°F for 5 to 10 minutes and test again.

Pork

Leaving New Orleans also frightened me considerably.
Outside of the city limits the heart of darkness, the true wasteland begins.

— *JOHN KENNEDY TOOLE,* A CONFEDERACY OF DUNCES

Because pigs and swine were easy to raise and maintain, they became a common food in the South. Referred to as cochon (cu-SHON), pork is right up there with chickens and seafood in Creole and Cajun cuisine. Perhaps the most common use of pork is making sausage. From boudin (rice and pork filled) to andouille (hamlike sausage), the links of south Louisiana are some of the best in the world. Sausage is used in most every gumbo and jambalaya, not to mention just eaten by itself.

But Louisiana cuisine is not limited to sausage. Pork chops or a good roast are at least once-a-week meals in Tremé. You can't beat Granny's oven-roasted pork roast smothered in the seasonings and spices of the area. One of my favorite Sunday dinners growing up was breaded pork chops, spicy greens, and a pot of white beans.

Kermit's Place

Want to experience some dyed-in-the-wool local authenticity? Mr. Ruffins, a local jazz trumpeter with a recurring cameo role on the *Tremé* series, now owns Kermit's Tremé Speakeasy at 1535 Basin Street. This jazzy joint, a soul food restaurant and clubhouse under the same roof, is an unpretentious real hangout for locals and tourists. Patrons are encouraged to visit for a spell with the man himself, when he's there cooking his famous recipes. You can even jam out with him on nights when he's playing there! So anyway you slice that cornbread, it's a win-win situation, y'all!

⤳ True Dat Breaded Pork Chops

Since our beloved Saints won the Super Bowl in 2010, New Orleanians have embraced the term "true dat" to represent our years and years of frustration before the triumph. It comes from an older phrase, "Who dat" (see page 94). With the Saints and our college teams, we do love our pigskin in Louisiana, along with a good old breaded and fried pork chop.

Serves 6

¼ cup canola oil
1 large egg, lightly beaten
½ cup milk
1 tablespoon All that Jazz Creole
and Cajun Blast (page 14)

2 cups crushed saltines
6 boneless pork loin chops, 1-inch
thick

Heat the oil in a large skillet over medium-high heat. In a shallow bowl, combine the egg and milk. Place the saltine crumbs in a second shallow bowl. Dip each pork chop in the egg mixture, then cover with saltine crumbs, patting to make a thick coating.

Cook the chops in the hot oil, turning once, until the meat is no longer pink, 8 to 10 minutes per side.

Willie Mae's Scotch House

One of the most famous restaurants in the Tremé is Willie Mae's Scotch House. It has been around since the mid-1950s and is famous for its fried pork chops, fried chicken, red beans and rice, and other traditional soul food dishes common to New Orleans. Willie Mae's is a stop you don't want to miss while visiting. Just try to get there early and be prepared to wait.

→ Lady Chevonne's Chitlins

Some recipes are called Southern, but the Creole and Cajun cultures cook differently from the rest of the South. Made from the intestines of the pig, chitlins are delicious if you can stand the smell of them while they are cooking. I suggest you make these on a cool day when you can open up the house, and put a halved onion in the pot while they boil to cut back on their pungent odor. They also need to be cleaned thoroughly to prevent food-borne illnesses, but it is a labor-intense process that can take hours. I suggest you buy them frozen and already cleaned. Check in the freezer section of your grocer or specialty meat market. Your butcher might even be able to get them for you fresh if you want to take the time to clean them. You can serve these with your favorite side dishes, such as greens, macaroni and cheese, or rice.

Serves 15 to 20 brave souls!

 10 pounds frozen cleaned chitlins (chitterlings), thawed
½ large white onion (optional)
2 cups Holy Trinity Wit da Pope (page 16)

2 teaspoons salt
1 teaspoon crushed red pepper
vinegar and hot sauce, to serve

Each chitlin should be examined and run under cold water; all foreign materials should be removed and discarded. Keep the chitlins soaking in cold water throughout the cleaning process. Chitlins should retain some fat, so be careful to leave some on.

After each chitlin has been cleaned, soak in a cold-water bath for 30 minutes. Drain the water and soak in a second cold-water bath for 30 minutes. The second water bath should be clearer. If not, soak once more.

Place the chitlins in a 6-quart pot and fill with cold water and bring to a boil over high heat. When the water is at a full boil, add the onion and Trinity with the salt and crushed red pepper. If the water is not boiling before adding the seasonings, your chitlins might become tough. Continue to simmer for 3 hours.

When serving, be sure to pass the vinegar and hot sauce.

Beef

We dance even if there's no radio. We drink at funerals. We talk too much and laugh too loud and live too large, and, frankly, we're suspicious of others who don't.

— CHRIS ROSE, 1 DEAD IN ATTIC

You can find a good steak almost anywhere in New Orleans. There are several dishes and techniques for cooking beef in the style of Tremé and the French Quarter that put a special twist on methods used elsewhere. The popular practice of blackening foods, developed by Chef Paul Prudhomme, was a natural for steaks. From the classic Southern chicken-fried steak with a little added heat to the classic French preparation of tripe, you'll find a resolution to your carnivorous cravings in this seafood capitol of cuisine.

Austin Leslie's Second Line

The second line that opens the premiere episode of the TV series *Tremé* re-creates a second line originally staged on October 9, 2005, in honor of Austin Leslie, a much-loved master of Creole soul food, who served as one of the inspirations for *Frank's Place*, a popular TV comedy series from the 1970s set in New Orleans. Leslie died in Atlanta, aged seventy-one, a few weeks after Hurricane Katrina.

→ Sidewalk Side Deep-Fried Tripe

Tripe is the edible parts of a cow's stomach, most well-known for its use in the classic Mexican soup menudo. Tripe may sound disgusting, but when fried up it has the chewy texture of calamari. My take on this surprisingly delicious finger food calls for deep-frying, which is so common along the Gulf Coast.

Serves 6

 3 tablespoons Suck da Heads and Pinch da Tails Creole Spice (page 13)

3 pounds beef tripe, cut into ¼-inch strips

vegetable oil, for frying
1 large egg
2 tablespoons barbecue sauce
1½ cups milk
2 cups all-purpose flour

Place the tripe and 2 tablespoons of the Creole spice in a large stockpot and add enough water to cover. Bring to a boil over high heat, then reduce the heat to medium-low, cover, and simmer for 1½ hours. Drain and rinse well with cold water. Drain again in a colander, squeezing out the excess water.

Pour vegetable oil into a deep-fryer or large, deep cast-iron pot to a depth of half the size of the fryer or pot. Heat the oil to 375°F. Line a large plate with paper towels.

In a medium bowl, beat together the egg, barbecue sauce, and milk. Stir in the flour, and mix until no dry lumps remain. Mix in the remaining tablespoon of spice. Dip the pieces of tripe into the egg batter and allow the excess to drip off. Carefully deep-fry the tripe in the hot oil until golden brown, about 2 minutes. Transfer to the paper towel–lined plate to drain. If you are frying the tripe in batches, spread the cooked pieces out on a large baking sheet and loosely cover with foil. Place the sheet in a preheated 200°F oven.

Sidewalk Side

So what does sidewalk side refer to? When you're at a Mardi Gras parade, you're either on the neutral ground side (the median) or the sidewalk side of the parade route. This is used by both parade goers and float riders to identify where on a float a masked rider might be located. If you know where your friend might be on a float, you can look for them and get extra-special throws.

One of the most visited events in the world every year is Carnival in New Orleans. Carnival starts right after Twelfth Night, on January 6, also known as Epiphany, and ends at midnight on Fat Tuesday (Mardi Gras). The following day, Ash Wednesday, marks the start of the Christian season of atonement known as Lent, the lead up to Easter.

Brought to the area by French settlers, the Mardi Gras holiday celebration was first held on March 3, 1699, at the mouth of the Mississippi River in Lower Plaquemines Parish. There is little agreement about when the current NOLA Mardi Gras season began. Some evidence suggests that the custom of holding Carnival balls began in the mid-1700s. What is certain is that the first official Mardi Gras parade in New Orleans rolled through the streets of the city in 1857, carried out by the Mystick Krewe of Comus, the first NOLA krewe. About twenty years later, Mardi Gras became a legal state holiday. To this day, it is the ultimate New Orleans experience and should be on everyone's bucket list.

⤳ Uncle Lionel's Chicken-Fried Steak

The practice of breading and frying cheap cuts of meat (much like frying chicken, hence the chicken-fried part) is common in the southern and western regions of the U.S. Variations on this dish are too many to count. Some folks prefer a cream gravy and others like a brown sauce. Some pan-fry the steak and others deep-fry it. My take on it adds a bit of hot sauce and garlic to make it true to the style of the Tremé. This steak goes great served with mashed potatoes and Zydeco Creole Green Beans (page 92).

Serves 4

3 cups vegetable shortening, for frying
4 (½-pound) beef cube steaks
2 cups plus ¼ cup all-purpose flour, divided
1 tablespoon All that Jazz Creole and Cajun Blast (page 14)
2 teaspoons baking powder
1 teaspoon baking soda

1 teaspoon black pepper
¾ teaspoon sea salt
1½ cups buttermilk
1 large egg
1 tablespoon Louisiana-style hot sauce
2 garlic cloves, minced
4 cups milk

Heat the shortening to 350°F in a deep cast-iron skillet. Line a large plate with paper towels. Pound the steaks to about ¼-inch thick. Place 2 cups of the flour in a shallow bowl and stir in the Creole and Cajun blast. In a second shallow bowl, stir together the baking powder, baking soda, pepper, and salt, then stir in the buttermilk, egg, hot sauce, and garlic.

Dredge each steak first in the flour, then in the batter, and again in the flour. Pat the flour onto the surface of each steak so they are completely coated with the dry flour. When the shortening is hot, fry the steaks until evenly golden brown, 3 to 5 minutes per side. Transfer the fried steaks to the paper towel–lined plate to drain.

Drain the fat from the skillet, reserving ¼ cup of the liquid and as much of the solid remnants as possible. Return the skillet to medium-low heat with the reserved oil. Whisk the remaining ¼ cup flour into the oil. Scrape the bottom of the pan with a spatula to release the solids into the gravy. Stir in the milk, raise the heat to medium, and bring the gravy to a simmer. Cook until thick, 6 to 7 minutes. Season with salt and pepper. Spoon the gravy over the steaks to serve.

→ Roxanne's Remarkable Roast

Sunday suppers often feature succulent roast beef as the main course. The addition of fresh garlic and flavorful Cajun spice adds a rustic flavor to the meat. Leftovers are good for sandwiches and salads. To complete the meal, serve petite new potatoes and green beans sautéed with bacon.

Serves 8 to 10

1 (4 to 5-pound) boneless beef roast
4 large garlic cloves, cut in half
   lengthwise (8 total pieces)
2 sprigs fresh thyme, cut into 1-inch
   pieces (8 total pieces)

4 teaspoons sea salt
1 teaspoon black pepper
Cajun dry rub
2 tablespoons olive oil
½ cup water

With the tip of a paring knife, make 8 slits in the beef roast at regular intervals about 1-inch deep. Slide a sliver of garlic and a sprig of thyme into each slit. Season with the sea salt, pepper, and a light dusting of Cajun dry rub. Place the meat in a zip-top bag or wrap with plastic wrap and refrigerate overnight.

Remove the beef from the refrigerator about 15 minutes before cooking. In an 8 to 10-quart Dutch oven, heat the oil over medium-high heat. Add the beef and brown on all sides. Turn the heat down to medium-low and add the water. Cover and simmer the beef until the meat is fork tender, about 4 hours. Throughout the cooking process, add small amounts of water, as needed. To serve, slice the beef against the grain and arrange on a serving dish on a bed of broad-leaf lettuce such as romaine.

❧ From the Grill

It is better to live here in sackcloth and ashes than own the entire state of Ohio.

—*LAFCADIO HEARN*

New Orleans cuisine is not known for barbecue or the smoked meat you'll find in Texas, Kansas City, Memphis, or the Carolinas. (But exceptions include the delicious smoked sausages and tasso used in many dishes here.) That said, there is a long tradition in south Louisiana of cooking whole pigs over an open fire pit. The Cochon de Lait festival is a popular celebration in Cajun areas of southwest Louisiana where the community celebrates the hog slaughters by roasting a suckling pig (a piglet fed only on its mother's milk) on a spit over an open fire. It's also not unusual in the streets of Tremé to enjoy the sweet, smoky smells of someone grilling meat on their barbecue pit. You'll also see billows of smoke around the football fields of New Orleans, where tailgating is an all-day event. Many of the local high schools in the city play their football games on Saturday, and of course on Sunday what's a Saints game without firing up your pit and grilling something under I-10?

How to Prepare Your Grill

For most of the following recipes, follow my basic technique for preparing your grill: heat one half of a gas grill to medium heat, about 435°F, or build a fire in one-half of a charcoal grill. I use natural lump coals, not briquettes, which have chemicals to help them burn; I don't like the taste of fuel on my food. Use enough coals to cover one side of your grill, which will last for one to four hours. I typically use a chimney starter (no lighter fluid needed) to fire up my coals. These are available most anywhere where they sell charcoal grills. A full chimney should work for most of these recipes, but you may need to add a few coals to rebuild the fire during the cooking process. When slow cooking (more than one hour), you will lose some heat toward the end, but that's OK. You can optionally add about 2 cups of your favorite water-soaked wood chips if you want to add a smoky flavor to your meat. A popular wood in south Louisiana is pecan. Soak the chips for about 30 minutes. You can use wood chips on a gas grill by wrapping them in foil, punching holes in the foil, and putting this packet directly on top of the heat source. There are also smoke boxes specially made for gas grills.

→ Xavier Char-Grilled Oysters

This one's a staple for summer barbecues and fall tailgate parties in south Louisiana. You can do this on your gas grill or over coals. The recipe below calls for oysters on the half shell, but I have also seen the oysters placed in their whole shells live on the grill. If you use oysters in whole shells, as they cook they will open up and they will be easy to eat right out of the shell with a butter sauce for dipping. Just make sure you clean the oysters good before you fire them up.

Serves 3 to 4

1 cup (2 sticks) unsalted butter
2 tablespoons finely chopped garlic
½ teaspoon black pepper
¼ cup grated Parmesan cheese

¼ cup grated Romano cheese
32 oysters, shucked, liqueur
    reserved on the half shell
½ cup finely chopped parsley

Fire up your grill to medium-high heat. Melt the butter with the garlic and pepper in a large skillet over medium heat. Combine the Parmesan and Romano cheeses in a small bowl. Spoon some of the melted butter sauce onto each oyster. Add a pinch of the cheese mixture and a pinch of parsley to each oyster, then place on the grill. Grill the oysters until they are hot, bubbly, and puffed up, about 8 minutes.

Kermit's BBQ Rig

One of the featured cameo appearances in the *Treme* television series is that of Kermit Ruffins, a popular NOLA musician, who is known for pulling his large black barbecue rig behind a large black truck and firing it up before he performs at a local venue. Ruffins is so well-known for these events that he named his backup band the Barbecue Swingers. You'll see Kermit in several scenes in *Treme* where he's cooking up grilled turkey necks right before a show. Check out Vaughn's Lounge in the Bywater neighborhood, where Kermit is known to play on Thursday nights and serve up his famous barbecue.

→ Leo of the Levee's Cedar-Smoked Redfish

For this recipe, you'll need a Northwest-style cedar smoking plank. I have always made this fish using a charcoal grill. You can use any type of firm fish with a fairly thick skin, such as red snapper or good-quality salmon.

Serves 2

1 large redfish fillet, with skin
1 medium green apple, thinly sliced
1 large lemon, thinly sliced
fresh basil leaves
½ cup (1 stick) butter, thinly sliced
lemon pepper

sea salt
paprika
leafy lettuce, for garnish
grilled lemon slices, for garnish
grilled apple slices, for garnish

Submerge a cedar plank in water and soak for at least 1 hour. Carefully remove the skin from the redfish, making sure that it remains in 1 piece, as you will be cooking the dish on it. You could ask your local fishmonger to do this for you.

When the cedar plank has soaked, place the fish skin on the plank scale-side down. Layer the apple, lemon, basil, and about ½ of the butter on the skin. Season the layers with a light coating of lemon pepper and sea salt. Lay the redfish on top of the layers. Season the top of the redfish with lemon pepper, sea salt, and paprika. Add the remaining butter slices to the top of the fish.

Prepare your fire using natural charcoal. You should have a hot-enough fire so that the plank will smoke. Once the coals are no longer flaming, place the plank with the fish on top of the grill directly over the fire. Wait a few minutes for the plank to start smoking. Once the plank is smoking nicely, cover the grill, making sure that it is vented above the flame.

Cooking times may vary depending on the size of the fish and your grill. The fish is done when it is firm to the touch, opaque, and flakes easily, or when the internal temperature is 140°F when tested with a meat thermometer. Carefully remove the plank from the grill and place it on a large metal serving tray. Garnish the tray with leafy lettuce, grilled lemon slices, and grilled apple slices.

✦ Mambo Beer Can Chicken

Also known as drunken chicken or beer-butt chicken, this easy style of preparation provides a simple way to make chicken melt in your mouth. Use a decent beer you like to drink, although amber ales tend to burn. My favorite is Abita Purple Haze, a raspberry beer produced in Louisiana. Cajun Injector Creole Butter is a name brand, but there are other decent products such as Tony Chachere's, which I've seen at grocers as far west as Colorado. You can prep the chicken with the injector butter and seasonings the night before cooking if you want; it will sit just fine in the refrigerator.

Serves 2 to 4

1 (4 to 6-pound) whole chicken
1 can good-quality beer
1 (16-ounce) jar Creole butter
   injector marinade or homemade
   substitute

2 ounces Creole/Cajun spice
2 teaspoons minced or crushed
   garlic

Pat the whole chicken dry (be sure to remove the giblets). With a flavor injector, inject the Creole butter or homemade substitute into all the meaty parts of the chicken. Some will ooze out—that's normal. In a small bowl, mix the Creole/Cajun spice with the garlic, then coat the chicken skin with the mixture. Prepare the grill as I have described in the introduction of this section.

You can also simply use the beer can to hold the chicken up. Or you can purchase a special wire rack that will support the chicken and hold a can of beer. Carefully place the cavity of the chicken over the beer can and set the chicken and beer on the grill but not directly over the heat source. Tent the top of the chicken with aluminum foil; this will keep the injector butter from steaming up through the chicken and burning. Cover or close the lid of the grill and open all air vents.

Cooking times will vary depending on your grill type and the coals you use (and a lot of other factors). You will need a meat thermometer to check doneness of the chicken. The internal temperature in the meaty part of the thigh and breast should be around 170°F when the chicken is done. When the leg moves easily in its socket that also indicates the chicken is ready. Note that the meat of the chicken will be pink when done, not white. This is typical of smoked chicken.

Carefully remove the chicken from the grill, and leave it on the beer can or rack to cool. Let stand for 10 to 15 minutes, and then carefully remove the chicken from the can or rack and cut it into pieces. Cook a couple of the side dishes mentioned earlier in this book. Just about anything goes well with this bird.

→ Purple Haze Pork Tenderloin

This pork recipe uses Abita Brewery's very popular Purple Haze beer, a delectable, raspberry-infused wheat brew. You can substitute other fruit-infused brews if you can't find Purple Haze.

½ cup (1 stick) unsalted butter
3 garlic cloves, crushed
¼ cup finely chopped red onion
¼ cup finely chopped red bell pepper
2 tablespoons chopped fresh basil
2 tablespoons All that Jazz Creole
    and Cajun Blast (page 14)

1 (12-ounce) bottle Abita Purple
    Haze beer, or other raspberry
    wheat beer
2 ounces Chambord liqueur
2 ounces agave nectar
2 to 3 (1-pound) pork tenderloins

To make the marinade, melt the butter in a medium saucepan over medium heat. Add the garlic, onion, bell pepper, basil, and Creole and Cajun blast, and cook, stirring, until the onions are translucent, about 7 minutes. Combine the Purple Haze, Chambord, and agave nectar in a blender or food processor, and add the sautéed vegetables. Purée until liquefied. Strain through a fine-mesh strainer or cheese cloth to make sure there are no small particles. Discard the solids and transfer the marinade to a flavor injector.

Prepare the tenderloins by injecting them with about half of the marinade. Place the tenderloins in a zip-top freezer bag and cover with the remaining marinade. Refrigerate for 1 hour.

Prepare the grill (see page 153). Place the pork directly over the fire and brown all sides. Baste the tenderloin with the marinade, then move the pork to the side of the grill with no fire or heat. I suggest you use wood chips on this recipe. Cover the grill, leaving the vents open, and cook the tenderloin, basting frequently, until the internal temperature is 160°F when checked with a meat thermometer.

Abita Beer

One of Louisiana's most popular microbreweries is Abita Brewing Company, in the small North Shore community of Abita Springs. They began brewing in 1986, and their award-winning brews are now available throughout the U.S. Not long after Hurricane Katrina, Abita produced Abita Restoration Ale and donated $1 from the sale of each six-pack toward hurricane recovery efforts.

Fall-Off-the-Bone Quick Pork Ribs

This rib recipe will take you less than an hour to make, and you won't believe how great it'll taste. The trick to quick ribs is to parboil them first in crab boil. Crab boil can be either liquid, powder, or a spice bag and is used in Louisiana to season boiled seafood. Many folks like to use crab boil when they boil potatoes and vegetables for added flavor as well. In fact, boil up some potatoes after you cook the ribs and use them for the Who Dat Potato Salad (page 90). This recipe works very well with beef ribs, too.

Serves 4 to 8

1 to 2 gallons water
1 cup crab boil
1 to 2-pound slab St. Louis–style pork ribs

Bring the water to a rapid boil in a large stockpot, stir in the crab boil, and boil for about 5 minutes. Add the ribs and parboil them for about 15 minutes. Turn off the heat and let the ribs stand in the water for about 20 minutes.

Prepare the grill (see page 153) while the ribs are parboiling and soaking. Once the coals are no longer flaming up, spread them out. Remove the ribs from the water and place on the grill. Brown the ribs on both sides. Remove the ribs and add a couple handfuls of your favorite wood chips. Do not soak the chips in water. Move the ribs to the other side of the grill and cover, making sure the top vent is open. Smoke the ribs for about 15 minutes. If you like your ribs wet (with sauce), brush on your favorite Louisiana-style barbecue sauce and caramelize directly over the fire. Be careful not to burn the sauce.

⤑ Congo Square Steak with Lump Crab Béarnaise Sauce

If you have a cooking partner in crime, they can make the sauce while you're cooking the steaks. This dish is excellent served with a nice Pinot Noir or a cold beer.

Serves 2

STEAK

8 to 16-ounce beef tenderloin, rib-eye steak, or New York strip steak (choice cut or above)
sea salt
black pepper

LUMP CRAB BÉARNAISE SAUCE

3 tablespoons white wine
1 tablespoon tarragon vinegar
2 teaspoons finely chopped fresh tarragon
2 tablespoons finely chopped chives
¼ teaspoon ground white pepper
½ cup (1 stick) unsalted butter
3 large egg yolks
2 tablespoons freshly squeezed lemon juice
¼ teaspoon sea salt
pinch cayenne pepper
½ pound fresh or packaged lump crabmeat (remove all shell fragments)

TO MAKE THE STEAK: Season the steaks with sea salt and pepper, and refrigerate for about 1 hour.

Build a fire in one half of a charcoal grill, or heat one half of a gas grill. Oil the grill grate or spray with cooking spray. Grill the steaks until they are 1 level below the desired doneness (e.g., for medium-rare steak, grill to rare).

TO MAKE THE SAUCE: Combine the wine, vinegar, tarragon, chives, and white pepper in a large saucepan over high heat. Bring to a rapid boil and cook until almost all the liquid disappears. In a small saucepan, heat butter until it bubbles, then remove from the heat. Do not allow the butter to brown! Combine the egg yolks, lemon juice, salt, and cayenne pepper in blender or food processor. Cover and pulse until smooth. Do not overblend. Gradually add the hot butter while blending at high speed. Add herb mixture, cover, and blend on high speed for 4 seconds. Pour the sauce into a large bowl, gently stir in the crab, and cover.

TO ASSEMBLE: When the sauce is ready, return the steaks to the grill to finish cooking to the desired doneness. Spoon the crab sauce over steaks right before serving.

Congo Square: Birthplace of Jazz

Congo Square was the town square of the Faubourg Tremé, a place where slaves were allowed to gather on Sundays to dance and play music and to conduct business, giving them opportunities to raise money to purchase their freedom.

African music was suppressed in the first colonies of the United States. As a result, Congo Square was a very popular destination for newcomers drawn here by this unique and exciting form of music. In particular, the music of Haitian refugees who flooded New Orleans during the early nineteenth century fused with the brass band sounds of the Tremé and led to the birth of American Dixieland jazz, which in turn influenced many other musical styles. Most of the jazz legends of New Orleans, such as Wynton Marsalis and Louis Armstrong, have ties to the Tremé area and Congo Square.

The jazz history of New Orleans takes center stage in the *Tremé* TV series, which often pits characters who play modern improvisational jazz against those who play the more traditional, African-influenced styles of New Orleans jazz music.

There's an interesting development on this front in the second season of *Tremé*, when Delmond Lambreaux, a successful modern jazz trumpet player in New York City and the son of Albert Lambreaux, Big Chief of a group of Mardi Gras Indians, blends the two styles to produce a fantastic hybrid of the modern and traditional sounds of jazz.

Desserts

Quick and Easy Classic Neighborhood

Desserts are like mistresses. They are bad for you.
So if you are having one, you might as well have two.

ALAIN DUCASSE

Just like the annual Southern Decadence celebration in September around Labor Day that is so popular in New Orleans, desserts in the Tremé neighborhood and around the city can be quite indulgent and festive. It's all about the flavors—luscious and satisfying! There's a time and a place for counting calories and watching waistlines, and that time and place is not while visiting the legendary Tremé.

✦ Immaculate White Chocolate Bread Pudding with Raspberry Sauce

This immaculate confection will fill you with sanctifying grace and tempt even the most ardent dieters out there.

 Serves 10 to 12

 BREAD PUDDING

4 cups heavy whipping cream

2 cups whole milk

1 cup sugar

3½ cups white chocolate chips

6 large eggs

12 large egg yolks

1 teaspoon vanilla extract

1 (24-inch) day-old French
baguette, cut into ½-inch slices

RASPBERRY SAUCE

½ cup water

½ cup sugar

2 teaspoons grated orange zest

2 cups fresh raspberries or 2 cups
frozen raspberries, thawed

 WHITE CHOCOLATE SAUCE

½ cup heavy whipping cream

1 cup white chocolate chips

 ASSEMBLY

5 tablespoons melted unsalted
butter

TO MAKE THE BREAD PUDDING: Preheat the oven to 325°F. Butter the bottom and sides of a 9 x 12-inch baking pan. Line the bottom of the pan with parchment paper.

Combine the cream, milk, and sugar in a large saucepan over medium heat and stir until hot. Add the white chocolate chips and stir until melted. Set aside to cool slightly.

In a large bowl, whisk the eggs, egg yolks, and vanilla to combine. To temper the eggs, pour a small amount of the cream mixture into the eggs and whisk to combine. You want to be sure that the cream mixture isn't too hot, or the eggs will scramble. Gradually whisk the remaining cream mixture into the egg mixture, and whisk until smooth.

Layer the pan with sliced bread and pour enough liquid to cover. Repeat this process until you have used all of the bread. Make sure the bread soaks up all of the liquid as you build each layer.

Cover the pan with foil and bake for 1 hour. After the first hour, remove the foil and continue to bake, uncovered, until it's no longer liquid in the center and the top is golden brown, about 30 minutes longer. While the bread pudding is baking, make the sauces.

TO MAKE THE RASPBERRY SAUCE: Combine the water, sugar, and orange zest in a medium saucepan over medium heat, and stir until the consistency is like syrup. Reduce the heat to low and add the raspberries, stirring occasionally, until the fruit falls apart, about 15 minutes. Pour the sauce through a fine-mesh strainer into a medium bowl to remove the seeds.

TO MAKE THE WHITE CHOCOLATE SAUCE: Heat the cream in a small saucepan over medium heat until hot. Stir in the white chocolate chips until melted. Set aside to cool slightly.

TO ASSEMBLE: When the bread pudding is cooked, cut into individual slices. Place the slices on a rimmed baking sheet and brush the top and sides of each slice with the melted butter. Bake until the outside is cripsy, 12 to 15 minutes. Drizzle with the white chocolate sauce and raspberry sauce.

Angelo Brocato's Original Italian Ice Cream Parlor

On the *Tremé* series, Creighton Bernette is a big fan of the ice cream at Angelo Brocato's Original Italian Ice Cream Parlor, a New Orleans landmark for more than a century. In the pilot episode, he turns down the lemon ice at a restaurant, professing his loyalty to Brocato's and vowing to not eat this favorite again until the popular shop reopens. In the first episode of season two, Creighton's wife and daughter, Toni and Sofia, are seen in line getting an icy treat in Brocato's and Arthur Brocato (the son of Angelo) makes a cameo appearance, talking with Toni about their reopening.

Brocato's, established in 1905, was affected badly by Katrina, taking on five feet of floodwater that resulted in the store's closure for more than a year. It seemed possible that the store might never reopen, so it's not surprising that there was a great deal of celebration among their loyal fans when it opened its doors again one year later in September 2006. When visiting NOLA, stop by 214 North Carrollton Avenue and taste why Brocato's reemergence was so anticipated.

→ Batiste Family Bread Puddin' with Praline Rum Sauce

So what do you do with that stale loaf of bread that's about to turn green? Well, in the Tremé they soak it in an egg mixture and then bake it as a lovely treat.

Serves 8 to 12

 BREAD PUDDING
- 8 (6-inch) loaves of stale French bread, cubed
- 5 large eggs, beaten
- 1 cup sugar
- ½ tablespoon ground cinnamon
- 5 cups milk
- 6 ounces (1½ sticks) unsalted butter
- 7 ounces crushed pineapple
- 2 teaspoons vanilla extract
- 1 (14-ounce) can condensed milk

 PRALINE SAUCE
- ¼ cup (½ stick) unsalted butter
- 1½ cups brown sugar, packed
- 2 cups heavy cream
- ¼ cup dark rum (spiced rum is good too!)
- 1 cup chopped pecans

TO MAKE THE BREAD PUDDING: Butter a 9 x 13-inch pan or baking dish, then spread the bread cubes in the pan.

In a large heatproof bowl, whisk together the eggs, sugar, and cinnamon. In a large saucepan over medium heat, combine the milk, butter, pineapple, vanilla, and condensed milk. Once the butter is completely melted in the milk mixture, stir to combine.

Remove from the heat and add a little of the milk mixture to the egg mixture, making sure the eggs do not scramble. Whisk to combine, then slowly whisk in the remaining milk mixture until it is completely combined. Pour the mixture over the bread and let it soak for 30 minutes. Preheat the oven to 350°F. Bake the bread pudding for 1 hour. You might want to put this on a baking sheet in case it bubbles over.

TO MAKE THE PRALINE SAUCE: Combine the butter and sugar in a medium saucepan and cook over low heat until the sugar is dissolved. Add the cream and bring to a simmer. Whisk in the rum, and add the pecans. Cook until the sauce is smooth, about 5 minutes longer. Pour the praline sauce over the cooked bread pudding and dish up.

→ Silly Sally's Slick-Tease Sorbet

This is my take on a popular refreshing mango freeze that is served at the New Orleans Jazz and Heritage Festival (aka Jazz Fest). The popular festival occurs in late April to early May and is more than a week of entertainment that reflects the diversity of New Orleans musical styles. If you don't have an ice cream maker, make the purée, put it in an airtight container, and freeze until firm. To make a simple syrup, combine equal parts water and sugar in a saucepan over medium heat, stir until the sugar dissolves, and cool to room temperature.

Serves 4 to 6

4 large mangoes or 32 ounces
    frozen mango chunks
3 tablespoons freshly squeezed lime
    juice
1 cup simple syrup or agave nectar

Chill the insert of an ice cream maker according to the manufacturer's instructions. Purée all the ingredients in a blender. Strain through a fine-mesh sieve into the cold bowl of the ice cream maker. Use a whisk to help push the pulp through. Freeze. Churn the purée in your ice cream maker until thick and creamy. Enjoy while listening to a good brass band! Freeze immediately (if there's any left).

Sno-Balls

A sno-ball isn't a snow-cone. It is not "shaved ice." Sno-balls are made from a finer, more snowlike ice than similar offerings in other cities. We loca-vores know: the New Orleans sno-ball is truly a unique specimen! In varieties as colorful as shotgun houses, Creole cottages, or Mardi Gras doubloons, with flavors like nectar cream (my favorite), spearmint, pink lemonade, and seemingly countless others, a sno-ball really does the trick for cooling you off on a summer day. There's also the option of adding condensed milk, or having your sno-ball "stuffed" with vanilla soft-serve ice cream.

We locals all have our favorite "stand" and often debate about which is best and why. Some of my favorites are: Hansen's Sno-Blitz Sweet Shop (4801 Tchoupitoulas Street), Sal's Snowballs (1823 Metairie Road in Metairie), Plum Street Snowballs (1300 Burdette Street), Pandora's Snowballs and Soft Serve Ice Cream (901 North Carrollton Avenue), and Papa Sam's Snowballs (2201 9th Street in Mandeville). And during the warmer months, Café Tremé opens its own sno-ball stand.

⤴ Pearl's Pecan Pralines with Bourbon and Brown Sugar

Pralines are confections that combine nuts and sugar for a scrumptious candy treat. They were brought to Louisiana by the French, and because sugar cane and pecans are so plentiful here, they have evolved into the modern-day pecan pralines. They differ from their European cousins in that they are made with heavy cream, and are softer, creamier, and more fudgelike.

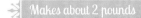 *Makes about 2 pounds*

5 tablespoons unsalted butter
1 cup granulated sugar
1 cup light brown sugar, packed
pinch salt
½ cup heavy cream

2 cups pecan halves, lightly toasted
2 teaspoons vanilla extract
1 tablespoon bourbon

Butter a rimmed baking sheet, or line with waxed paper. In a large, heavy saucepan over low heat, melt 4 tablespoons of the butter. Stir in the granulated sugar, brown sugar, salt, and cream. Cover, increase the heat to medium, and bring to a boil.

Remove the lid and attach a candy thermometer to the pan. Boil until the temperature of the mixture reaches 242°F on the candy thermometer, or until a small amount of the mixture, when added to cold water, forms a soft ball. Mix in the toasted pecans. Remove from the heat and whisk in the vanilla and bourbon. Continue beating until the candy becomes creamy, and begins to thicken.

Quickly drop the candy mixture by tablespoons onto the prepared baking sheet. Allow the candy to cool to room temperature until it is firm to the touch. Each praline can be stored, wrapped individually in plastic wrap.

⇥ Your Gay Best Friend's Mardi Gras King Cake Cupcakes with Flamboyant Cinnamon-Mascarpone Frosting

New Orleans has a prominent gay population and tourist industry that are active in the community. The biggest event of the community's year is a festival called Southern Decadance (see page 201), also known as Gay Mardi Gras. This recipe is a cupcake rendition of the famous king cake that is a big part of all pre–Mardi Gras events, which has a small trinket, usually a baby, hidden somewhere inside. You can hide the baby in one of the cupcakes; just make sure you let everyone know that the baby is there so that no one swallows it, or worse, chokes on it.

 Makes 12

CUPCAKES
1 (18.25-ounce) box yellow or
    butter-flavored cake mix
1 cup buttermilk
⅓ cup vegetable oil
4 large eggs
½ cup brown sugar, packed
1 tablespoon ground cinnamon
2 tablespoons unsalted butter,
    melted

FROSTING
1 cup cold heavy whipping cream
8 ounces mascarpone cheese
½ tablespoon ground cinnamon
2 to 3 cups confectioners' sugar
    (depending upon how thick you
    like your icing)

ASSEMBLY
purple-, yellow-, and green-colored
    sugar

FOR THE CUPCAKES: Preheat the oven to 350°F and line 12 standard muffin cups with paper liners. In a large bowl, combine the cake mix, buttermilk, oil, and eggs. In a separate small bowl, stir together the brown sugar and cinnamon. Add the melted butter, and stir until crumbly.

Using a cookie dough scoop, spoon about 1 tablespoon of the cake batter into each prepared muffin cup. Evenly sprinkle with the cinnamon mixture and add 2 tablespoons more of the cake batter to each cup. Bake until a toothpick inserted in the center comes out clean, about 15 minutes. Cool completely on a wire rack.

FOR THE FROSTING: In a stand mixer fitted with the whip attachment, or in a large bowl with a handheld mixer, whip the cream until soft peaks begin to form. Fold in the mascarpone cheese, then mix in the cinnamon. With the mixer running, slowly add about 2 cups of the confectioners' sugar, being careful not to overwhip the frosting or to make it too thick. The frosting should be thin enough to drizzle on top of the cake (or cupcakes), but if you'd like the frosting thicker, mix in up to 1 cup more confectioners' sugar.

FOR ASSEMBLY: Spoon the frosting over the middle of the each cupcake and let it drip down the sides. Immediately sprinkle with purple-, yellow-, and green-colored sugar.

Mardi Gras King Cake

King cake season runs from Epiphany (twelve days after Christmas) up until Fat Tuesday (Mardi Gras), the day before the start of Lent. It's common to have weekly king cake gatherings at work or with friends during this period of time. King refers to the biblical three kings, from the biblical telling of the birth of Christ. In a practice dating back to the 1930s, a small baby, symbolizing the baby Jesus, is hidden within the cake, and whoever gets the baby is tasked with supplying the cake at the next Mardi Gras gathering.

The traditional king cake has purple, green, and gold granulated sugar sprinkled on top of the cake to represent the colors of Mardi Gras. In 1892, the colors were selected by Rex, the King of the Krewe of Rex, one of the most prominent and attended parades on Fat Tuesday, and they have special meaning during Carnival time. The purple stands for justice, the green for faith, and the gold for power. Variations on the traditional cake have grown in recent years, and now many bakers are including a filling such as cream cheese, cinnamon, or fruit jam. Perhaps one of the most interesting (and delicious, I might add) is the Zulu King Cake, which is filled with coconut and topped with a chocolate icing.

→ Chocolate City Sin Cake

On Martin Luther King Day, January 16, 2006, New Orleans Mayor Ray Nagin made his famous and controversial "Chocolate City" speech. Many interpreted the speech as a condemnation of the prominently caucasian population that was returning to the city. He later apologized and clarified his statements as meaning that New Orleans has a diverse population in which white and black residents mix and blend together to make the city flourish. Many local pundits said his political career was over, but he won reelection and served his last term until 2010.

Serves 10 to 15

4 cups (32 ounces) chocolate chips
2½ cups plus 2½ tablespoons
   (5⅓ sticks) salted butter, cut
   into pieces
⅔ cup water

2 cups sugar
16 eggs
ice cream or whipped cream,
   for topping

Preheat oven to 350°F. Pour 1 inch of water into a 3-inch-deep pan and place on a low rack to create steam while the cake bakes in the oven. Spray 2 (5 x 9-inch) loaf pans with cooking spray and then coat with flour.

Melt the chocolate chips and butter in a double boiler over medium heat. Heat the water in a medium saucepan and add the sugar, stirring until it dissolves. Whisk this into the melted chocolate until the mixture is smooth. Remove from the heat and allow the mixture to cool for about 2 minutes. Lightly beat the eggs and whisk into the chocolate mixture.

Pour the cake batter evenly into the prepared pans. Bake for about 1 hour. Test the cake every 5 minutes after the hour by inserting a toothpick. When no batter clings to the toothpick, the cake is done. Turn the oven off and let the cake stand in the oven for 1 hour. Remove and let cool completely in the pans on a wire rack. Carefully remove the cakes from the pans. Slice, and top each piece with your favorite ice cream or whipped cream. I like amaretto whipped cream, myself. Just add 1 tablespoon of amaretto to 1 pint of heavy cream, and whip.

✦ Joie de Vivre Heavenly Hash Cake

This one was recommended by a close friend from Uptown NOLA. She got it from her mother, who got it from hers, who got it from...well, you get the picture. *Joie de vivre* means "the joy of life," and after you take a bite of this cake, you'll understand our joy in New Orleans.

 Serves 4 to 8

CAKE
4 eggs, lightly beaten
2 cups sugar
1 cup (2 sticks) unsalted butter
1½ cups self-rising flour
2 cups Louisiana pecans, chopped
1 teaspoon vanilla extract
2 tablespoons unsweetened cocoa
    powder, divided

ICING GLAZE
1 (16-ounce) bag miniature
    marshmallows (about 2 cups)
4 teaspoons unsweetened cocoa
    powder
½ cup (1 stick) butter, melted
1 pound confectioners' sugar
2 tablespoons plus 2 teaspoons
    evaporated milk

TO MAKE THE CAKE: Preheat the oven to 350°F. Combine the eggs, sugar, butter, flour, pecans, vanilla, and cocoa in a large bowl. Mix well. Pour into an ungreased 9 x 13-inch baking pan and bake until a toothpick inserted in the center comes out clean, about 40 minutes. Allow to cool completely.

TO PREPARE THE ICING GLAZE: Arrange the marshmallows on top of the cooled cake. Broil until the marshmallows are melted, 1 to 3 minutes, watching closely to be sure they don't burn. In a medium saucepan over medium heat, mix the cocoa, butter, confectioners' sugar, and evaporated milk and heat until the icing is a spreadable consistency. Spread over the marshmallows. Allow the icing to set. Cut into squares to serve.

Elmer Chocolates

Heavenly Hash Eggs are made by the Elmer Chocolate company, founded in 1855 in New Orleans. They are now famous primarily for their seasonal chocolate boxes (Christmas, Valentine's, and Easter), but they still produce their classic individually wrapped candies Gold Brick, Heavenly Hash, and Pecan Egg during Easter. First produced in 1923, Heavenly Hash is the oldest of the three. These candies are sold throughout the States along the Gulf Coast at many retail stores, drug stores, and grocers.

⤳ Dorgenois Street Buttermilk Drops

These tasty little fried pastries are a NOLA favorite. Ask anyone who returned to the city during the first year after Katrina what they missed the most, and I'd bet they'll say buttermilk drops. About the size of a doughnut hole, these treats are addictive.

Serves 4 to 6

- vegetable oil, for frying
- 2 cups all-purpose flour
- ¼ cup sugar
- 1 teaspoon salt
- 1 teaspoon baking powder
- ¾ teaspoon baking soda
- 1 teaspoon ground nutmeg
- ¼ cup vegetable oil
- ¾ cup buttermilk
- 1 egg
- 1 cup confectioners' sugar

Pour 3 to 4 inches of oil into a large, deep cast-iron pot. Heat to 365°F. You can also fry these in a deep fryer.

Mix the flour, sugar, salt, baking powder, baking soda, and nutmeg in a large bowl. In a medium bowl, whisk together the oil, buttermilk, and egg. Beat the wet ingredients into the dry ingredients until smooth.

Cover a large rimmed baking dish with paper towels. Using a regular teaspoon or a ½ to ¾-inch melon baller, drop the batter into the oil, being careful not to crowd the pan. Fry until golden brown, about 3 to 4 minutes, stirring frequently to make sure they cook evenly. Drain well on the paper towels and immediately shake the confectioners' sugar on top while they are hot. Toss the pan and apply more confectioners' sugar until all sides are covered.

The Buttermilk Drop Bakery

There has traditionally been a bakery on almost every corner of the city, and many have reopened post-Katrina. One of the most popular is Dwight Henry's Buttermilk Drop Bakery. Mr. Henry began his career in the Lower Ninth Ward and worked at several bakeries over a span of two decades before he opened his own shop. His original location was severely damaged by Katrina, and there was some apprehension on his part about whether to open again. Fortunately, he missed baking so much that he reopened to block-long lines. Located in Tremé at 1781 North Dorgenois Street, this is a must for anyone visiting the city. Stop by and enjoy the buttermilk drops or a hot breakfast or lunch. I promise you won't be disappointed.

✦ McKenzie's Turtle Cookies

A New Orleans tradition for over 70 years, McKenzie's Bakery closed in 2001. These are the best cookies on earth, y'all.

COOKIES
2 eggs, divided
½ cup (1 stick) butter or margarine
½ cup light brown sugar, packed
¼ teaspoon vanilla extract
1 teaspoon maple flavoring
1½ cups all-purpose flour
¼ teaspoon salt
¼ teaspoon baking soda
pecan halves

FROSTING
2 ounces semisweet baking
  chocolate
¼ cup milk
1 tablespoon unsalted butter
1 pound confectioners' sugar

TO MAKE THE COOKIES: Separate 1 of the eggs. In a large bowl, cream the butter with the sugar until light and fluffy. Beat in the remaining whole egg and the egg yolk, vanilla, and maple flavoring. Set aside.

In a medium bowl, sift together the flour, salt, and baking soda. Gradually add the dry ingredients to the creamed mixture until you have a smooth dough. Cover with a moist towel and refrigerate for 2 hours.

Preheat the oven to 350°F. Spray a rimmed baking sheet with cooking spray. Arrange the pecans in groups of 5 on the baking sheet.

Shape the dough into 1-teaspoon balls, then shape them to be ovals, like a turtle body. Dip the bottoms into a little of the egg white. Press slightly onto the prepared baking sheet on the groups of pecan halves to form the head and 4 feet of the turtles.

Bake until the cookies are done, 10 to 12 minutes. Allow to cool on a rack or in the pan for 20 to 30 minutes.

TO MAKE THE FROSTING: In a large saucepan over medium-low heat, melt the chocolate with the milk and butter. Beat in the powdered sugar until smooth. Frost the cookies when they are completely cool.

→ Betina's Blackberry Cobbler

Betina is a friend of a friend who lived in the Seventh Ward, not too far from the Tremé, and has been baking this delightful cobbler for years. What makes this so special are the berries she picked from the trellis she tended for years in her small backyard. Unfortunately, Betina lost her home and beloved berries in the storm and hasn't returned to the city. Last I heard, she was living in Georgia and was growing blackberries again.

2 cups white sugar
2 tablespoons cornstarch
6 cups fresh blackberries
½ cup unsalted butter, melted
2½ cups all-purpose flour

1 tablespoon baking powder
1 teaspoon salt
2 cups whole milk
1 tablespoon vanilla extract
vanilla ice cream, to serve

Preheat the oven to 350°F. Lightly butter a 9 x 13-inch baking dish. Stir together ½ cup of the sugar with the cornstarch in a small bowl and set aside. Wash the blackberries and place them in a large bowl and drizzle with ¼ cup of the melted butter. Sprinkle with the cornstarch mixture, and toss to evenly coat. Spread the berries in the prepared baking dish.

In a medium bowl, mix together the flour, remaining 1½ cups sugar, baking powder, and salt, until evenly blended. Stir in the milk, vanilla extract, and remaining ¼ cup melted butter until combined but still slightly lumpy. Pour the batter over the blackberries.

Bake in the preheated oven until the berries are tender and the crust is golden brown, about 1 hour. Cool for about 30 minutes. Serve with a nice vanilla bean ice cream.

→ Party Gras Peach Crisp

If you're visiting the Tremé, you'll find the best peach cobbler on earth at the famed Dooky Chase Restaurant. My cousin's peach crisp is pretty damn good too, and I am sharing her recipe with you.

Serves 8 to 12

1½ cups sugar, or more if you like it
   sweeter
1 tablespoon cornstarch
¼ teaspoon ground cinnamon
4 cups sliced fresh peaches (about 6
   medium peaches)

1 teaspoon freshly squeezed lemon
   juice
1 large egg
1 cup all-purpose flour
6 tablespoons unsalted butter, melted
vanilla ice cream, to serve

Preheat the oven to 375°F. Stir together ½ cup of the sugar, the cornstarch, and the cinnamon in a large saucepan. Stir in the peaches and lemon juice. Cook over medium heat, stirring constantly, until the mixture thickens and boils. Boil and stir for 1 minute. Pour into ungreased 2-quart casserole dish.

In a medium bowl, stir together the egg, flour, and remaining 1 cup of sugar until the mixture resembles coarse meal. Sprinkle over the peaches. Drizzle the melted butter over the topping.

Bake until lightly browned and bubbly, about 45 minutes. Let stand for 15 minutes. Serve with a scoop of vanilla ice cream.

Dooky Chase

A cornerstone of the Tremé neighborhood is Dooky Chase (2301 Orleans Avenue), a white-tablecloth restaurant that was a center for the Civil Rights movement during the mid-1960s. Chef and co-owner Leah Chase was one of the first restaurateurs to reopen her business after Hurricane Katrina, with the help of many former customers. Chef Chase, la grande dame of Creole cooking, still makes time to walk around and greet her customers, as they help themselves to the delectable buffet of sweet corn succotash, spicy gumbo, fried chicken, catfish, and collard greens (to name but a few of the offerings). Oh, and don't forget that peach cobbler for dessert! On my last visit, Ms. Leah came into the room and made her rounds, as usual. I asked her to sit down, and she smirked, "They'd fire me. You know how they do with us old people." In the show *Tremé*, Chef Chase even makes a cameo appearance in scenes that were filmed at this eatery.

Cocktails

Let him drink, and forget his poverty, and remember
his misery no more.

PROVERBS 31:7

"Somebody puts something in front of you here and you
might as well drink it. Great place to be intimate or do
nothing. A place to come and hope you'll get smart—to
feed pigeons looking for handouts."

BOB DYLAN, CHRONICLES, VOL. 1

Cocktails act like a liquid medication to calm the nerves and improve the mood, and in New Orleans, you'll find some of the best mixed drinks on the planet. In fact, history suggests that the cocktail as we know it evolved right here in the Crescent City at a local pharmacy, and we celebrate that fact with our very own Museum of the American Cocktail (see page 188).

We're still perfecting the art form here in the city that's famous not only for its original cuisine but for its nightlife and music. There's always an excuse for a good party in NOLA, always a festival to celebrate, another excuse to get outdoors for us humid-beings! And when it's hot, what better way to cool down, than with a refreshing, cool adult beverage. Enjoy a Hurricane, a Sazerac, a Vieux Carré, or any of the other libations made famous in the Big Easy! Cheers!

→ Mardi Gras Molotov Cocktail

Mardi Gras is a very libatious experience involving a lot of celebratory drinking, and this cocktail might be just the thing to get you going. Careful though—one of these packs a pretty big bang and you may not even know you are drinking something so strong. Many states have banned the sale of 190-proof Everclear (190-proof means 95% alcohol), and some don't even allow the sale of the 151-proof; if you can't find it, just use the highest-proof vodka you can get. I once saw a guy doing a shot that was topped with flaming 190, and when he went to down the drink before the fire went out, his upper lip went up in flames. Of course, he didn't feel a thing!

Serves 1 sober person!

1 ounce amaretto liqueur
1 ounce good-quality rum
1 ounce melon liqueur

2 ounces 190-proof Everclear
pineapple juice
ice

Fill a tall Collins glass halfway with amaretto. Add the rum, melon liqueur, and Everclear. Fill up the glass the rest of the way with pineapple juice. Stir. Pour into a large hurricane glass over crushed ice.

The Museum of the American Cocktail

This is a must-see if you are a mixologist or just a connoisseur of fine libations. If you are there at the right time, you may be able to catch one of their events or seminars, featuring some of the best bartenders in the city. The non-profit museum's mission statement says that they want to create an attraction that celebrates the art of the cocktail and provides resources for professional mixologists, while emphasizing the importance of responsible drinking. For more information, visit www.museumoftheamericancocktail.com.

→ Crabby's Creole Bloody Mary

All things New Orleans are a little spicy, so why would our cocktails be any different? Whether served alongside Sunday brunch, at cocktail hour, or long after the sun has set across the Mississippi, these Bloody Marys are a very New Orleans beverage. If you sipped a few too many spirited New Orleans concoctions the evening before, a Bloody Mary will bring you back to life.

Makes 4 to 8 drinks

1 cup vodka
4½ cups cold tomato juice
2 tablespoons freshly squeezed lime
    juice
1 tablespoon Worcestershire sauce
4 to 6 dashes Tabasco hot sauce

celery salt and black pepper
for garnish: try pickled okra, pickled
    green beans, giant olives, celery
    stalks, and lime slices (mix or
    match to your satisfaction)

Combine all the ingredients in a container with a lid. Do not add ice. Shake vigorously. Pour the mixture over ice cubes in pint glasses. Use the garnish of your choice. You can mix this up the night before your party and refrigerate. The flavors will become more pronounced when they have a little time to steep with the vodka.

↔ Krewe Dat Carnival Martini

This martini uses recent products developed by Absolut that infuse vodka with mangoes and black pepper. Very NOLA!

Serves 1

1½ ounces Absolut Pappar Vodka
1½ ounces Absolut Mango Vodka
½ ounce simple syrup
squeeze lime juice
½ ounce grenadine

½ ounce sweet-and-sour mix
purple-, green-, and gold-colored
     sugars, for rimming the glass
maraschino cherry, for garnish

Pour the vodka, simple syrup, lime juice, grenadine, and sweet-and-sour mix over ice in a cocktail shaker. Shake vigorously. Sugar the rim of a large martini glass with the Mardi Gras–colored sugars. Strain the cocktail into the glass and garnish with a cherry.

Mardi Gras Krewes

"Krewe" is a term that is given to the social organizations that sponsor balls and parades during Carnival season (Mardi Gras). Members of these groups pay fees ranging from a few dollars to thousands to belong to the organizations and participate in the activities they sponsor. Of course, the higher the membership fees, the grander the events and floats. Some famous krewes include the Mistick Krew of Comus, Rex, and the Zulu Social Aid and Pleasure Club.

In the *Tremé* episode "All on a Mardi Gras Day," the 2006 Mardi Gras festival is featured—an event that many New Orleanians believe symbolizes the true beginnings of the revival of the city. Some residents were critical of city officials for even considering having Carnival that year, so soon after Katrina. But the flame of Mardi Gras could not be dampened and the parades were allowed to go ahead, helping to bring about healing for the storm-weary city.

✦ Esplanade Mint Julep

The first printed description of the mint julep in 1803 described the drink as "a dram of spiritous liquor that has mint steeped in it, and is taken by Virginians of a morning." Its origins are hazy, but when it comes right down to it, this refreshing and potent sultry summer beverage is just as at home in the Tremé as it is trackside on Kentucky Derby Day. The mint julep has found a home in many bars and restaurants across the city.

Serves 1

4 sprigs fresh mint
1 to 2 tablespoons sugar
1 tablespoon water

crushed ice
2 ounces bourbon

In a tall Collins glass, muddle the mint with the sugar. Add the water and stir until the sugar dissolves. Fill the glass to the top with crushed ice. Add the bourbon to the top of the glass.

✦ The New Orleans Sidecar

This classic cocktail is served in fine higher-end bars worldwide. Commander's Palace, one of the best restaurants in NOLA, located at 1403 Washington Avenue, is well-known for serving sidecars in the classic style. The blog Go NOLA (www.gonola.com) lists this drink as "a delicious and unique-to-New Orleans cocktail" and suggests the version at Commander's Palace as the best, in a post from April 2011, "It's Five O'Clock Somewhere: Five New Orleans Cocktails."

Serves 1

2 tablespoons superfine sugar
1 lemon wedge
2 ounces brandy or cognac
1 ounce orange liquor

ice
½ ounce freshly squeezed lemon
  juice
1 lemon twist

Spread the superfine sugar on a plate. Moisten the rim of a martini glass with the lemon wedge and dip the rim into the sugar. Place the glass in the freezer for about an hour before you make the cocktail.

Combine the brandy or cognac and orange liquor in a mixing glass with the lemon juice. Add ice and shake vigorously. Remove the martini glass from the freezer, twist the lemon over the glass, and drop it into the bottom. Strain the liquor into the cold martini glass.

✛ Gris-Gris (Category-5) Hurricane Punch

Gris-gris (pronounced gree-gree) are amulets or incantations used to cast spells in voodoo, the African folk religion that is intertwined with the history of New Orleans. This drink is so-called because you may feel like someone has put a spell on you. Hurricanes have a strange effect on people. Just sit outside Pat O'Brien's, where this cocktail was invented, and watch folks come out the door. They often don't know what hit them. Perhaps it's all that rum that they put in the drink.

Serves 1

crushed ice
1½ ounces light rum
pineapple juice
orange juice
cranberry juice

maraschino cherries, with juice
2 ounces dark rum
lemon wedges and other fruit,
   garnish

Fill a hurricane glass with crushed ice. Add the light rum. Fill the glass with equal parts pineapple, orange, and cranberry juice, stopping about 1 inch from the top of the glass. Pour a splash of maraschino cherry juice on top. Float the dark rum on top of the drink by pouring slowly over the back of a bar spoon or teaspoon. Do not stir! Garnish with lemon slices, cherries, or any other fresh fruit.

✛ The Vieux Carré Cocktail

This drink was invented in 1938 by Walter Bergeron, head bartender at the Monteleone Hotel in New Orleans. It is named for the French term for what we call the French Quarter: le Vieux Carré (Old Square).

Serves 1

1 ounce rye whiskey
1 ounce cognac
1 ounce sweet vermouth
1 teaspoon Bénédictine D.O.M.

2 dashes Peychaud's bitters
2 dashes angostura bitters
ice

Mix all the ingredients in a double old-fashioned glass over ice. Stir and enjoy.

New Orleans Voodoo

New Orleans voodoo originated during the days of slave trading and blends the traditions of Afro-American religions with the French, Spanish, and Creole Catholic traditions of New Orleans. It has its roots in Catholic-infuenced Caribbean West African ancestor-worship practices (Vodou and Santeria), emphasizing animal sacrifice, trance states, and the use of charms or amulets, poisons, and herbs for self-protection or to do harm to enemies. These found their way to Louisiana when Haitian refugees were forced to flee their country during the Haitian revolution at the end of the 1700s. The practice of voodoo is still around in the Tremé. In the first episode of season 2 of the HBO series *Tremé*, there is a brief scene in what is probably Saint Louis Cemetery, with priestesses performing a voodoo candle-lighting ritual.

New Orleans voodoo emphasizes grisgris (charms and spells), voodoo queens (priestesses), the use of occult paraphernalia (voodoo dolls), and the Li Grand Zombi (snake deity). Probably the best-known voodoo practice is that of sticking a pin in a voodoo doll to cause pain to a rival.

The most popular voodoo queen was Marie Laveau, a free woman of color who practiced voodoo and had a strong following in the 1830s. A devout Catholic, Laveau also suggested that her followers attend Mass every Sunday—and who was going to argue with Queen Laveau? Her tomb in Saint Louis Cemetery (see page 21) is a popular tourist site, visited by thousands every year, not only out of curiosity but also to ask favors from the famous voodoo queen.

⤳ Henry's Ramos Fizz

This famous cocktail, often served during Sunday brunch, was invented in New Orleans and makes for a sprightly pick-me-up. Don't worry about drinking something containing raw eggs: part of the reason for the long minutes of shaking the drink is to make sure that the alcohol "cooks" the egg white.

Serves 1

1½ ounces gin
½ ounce freshly squeezed lime juice
½ ounce freshly squeezed lemon
   juice
1¼ ounces simple syrup
2 ounces heavy cream

1 small egg white
2 dashes fleurs d'orange (orange
   flower water)
ice
soda water

Pour all the ingredients except the ice and soda water into a cocktail shaker. Shake vigorously for several minutes to ensure the egg and cream are blended well. This will take several minutes, so make sure you stretch those arm muscles well before you start! Add ice and shake a bit more. Strain into a chilled Collins glass. Top with the soda water.

The Ramos Fizz

The Ramos Fizz is named for Henry Ramos, who invented it in his bar, the Cabinet Saloon, in 1888. Time consuming to make, at one time the cocktail was so popular that Henry had to hire twenty bartenders to keep up with demand. I have known many a bartender who hated making this cocktail. It's the separating the eggs part they most despise and it's time consuming during a busy Sunday brunch.

→ Verdie Mae's Absinthe Frappé

A frappé is commonly thought of as frozen dessert made with shaved ice and is often associated with cold coffee beverages. However, it's also a method of mixing cocktails that involves pouring sweet liqueurs over shaved ice. The mint julep could be considered a type of frappé. This is my take on a classic julep, using absinthe instead of bourbon to give it a distinct New Orleans character.

Serves 1

6 to 8 mint leaves
2 teaspoons granulated sugar
1½ ounces absinthe

mint sprig, for garnish
2 ounces soda water
crushed ice

Muddle the mint leaves and sugar in a tall Collins glass. Pour in the absinthe and stir until the sugar dissolves, then fill the glass with crushed ice. Top with splash of soda, and garnish with a sprig of mint.

Absinthe

So have you heard that absinthe will cause blindness or can lead to time in a padded cell? This green-colored spirit derived from herbs is high in alcohol by volume and was banned in Europe and the U.S. by 1912 because it was allegedly an addictive psychoactive drug harmful for human consumption. It has recently been determined that absinthe contains little of the chemical thujone, a hallucinogenic, and you can now purchase a slightly altered version that does not contain this ingredient in the United States. Europe allows the chemical but regulates the amount to safe levels. Traditionally, absinthe is prepared by pouring cold water over a sugar cube into a shot. Verdi Mae's Absinthe Frappé is how I enjoy drinking this "forbidden" libation.

→ Janette Desautel's Right in Your Face Sazerac

One of my favorite scenes in the *Tremé* series is when Alan Richman, a real-life prominent food writer, has a Sazerac very skillfully thrown in his face by aspiring chef Janette Desautel. If you are not familiar with Mr. Richman's work, he did a thorough bashing of post-Katrina New Orleans in a November 2006 article for *GQ* magazine criticizing the food and culture of the city. This upset many people who were working hard in the recovery efforts. Some say that Richman was trying to make amends by making a cameo appearance in this episode and allowing the drink of New Orleans to be thrown at his ugly mug.

 Serves 1

1 tablespoon sugar
4 dashes Peychaud's bitters
3 ounces rye whiskey
cubed ice, as needed

absinthe or the absinthe substitute Herbsaint or a French pastis
lemon twist, for garnish

Chill an old-fashioned glass by filling it with crushed ice and letting it sit while you prepare the rest of the drink.

In a separate mixing glass, muddle the sugar with the Peychaud's bitters. Add the rye whiskey, and stir until the sugar is dissolved. Fill the glass with cubed ice and stir until well chilled. Discard the ice in the cold old-fashioned glass and rinse it with absinthe by pouring a small amount into the glass, swirling it around and making sure the entire inside of the glass is coated, and then discard any excess.

Strain the whiskey mixture from the mixing glass into the cold old-fashioned glass. Twist a lemon peel over the glass and discard. Traditionally the twist is not dropped into the glass.

History of the Sazerac

The Sazerac is unique to New Orleans and is sometimes called the oldest cocktail in America. There are several legends about the drink's creation. One says that it was invented in 1850 by Aaron Bird, owner of the Sazerac House, who began serving a cocktail combining imported Sazerac de Forge et Fils cognac with Peychaud's bitters, which, legend has it, were made in a drug store down the street by a Creole apothecary (now known as a pharmacist) from the West Indies, Antoine Amadie Peychaud.

Another story has it that Peychaud himself invented the Sazerac, using his proprietary mix of aromatic bitters from an old family recipe. According to legend, Peychaud served his drink in the large end of an egg cup, called a *coquetier* in French. The Americanized pronunciation of this sounded like "cocktail," giving this type of drink its name. This tale has been debunked after references to the word "cocktail" have been found in writings from the very early nineteenth century.

✦ Voulez-Vous Coucher avec Moi Ce Soir? Daiquiri

This multicolored, layered daiquiri recipe comes from a drag queen in the Tremé who claims to be the original Creole Lady Marmalade! Its layers match the colors of Mardi Gras—purple, gold, and green—and it's a must for any home Mardi Gras party. Serve it with a straw, and drink slowly or you'll get brain freeze.

Serves 2

2 ounces light rum, divided
2 ounces frozen sliced strawberries
2½ ounces blue curaçao, divided
2 ounces sweet-and-sour mix, divided

2 cups crushed ice, divided
3 ounces fresh mango, chopped
1 ounce freshly squeezed lime juice

Start by making the purple portion of the daiquiri. Pour 1 ounce of the light rum, the strawberries, 2 ounces of the blue curaçao, 1 ounce of the sweet-and-sour mix, and 1 cup of the ice into a blender and purée. Pour into a tall glass. Rinse out the blender container.

To make the gold portion of the drink, pour the remaining 1 ounce of rum, the mango, the remaining 1 ounce of sweet-and-sour, and the remaining 1 cup of ice into a blender and purée. Pour half the mixture into the glass, on top of the purple purée, and reserve the rest.

To create the green portion of the drink, blend the remaining gold mixture purée with the remaining ½ ounce of blue curaçao and the lime juice in the blender, and pour into the glass over the gold mixture.

Drive-Through Daiquiris

Yes, it's legal in Louisiana to drive up to a window and purchase an individual frozen daiquiri or even a gallon to-go at "daiquiri joints." You may ask, don't they have open-container laws in Louisiana? They do, but there's a stipulation in the law that exempts the frozen daiquiri as long as it is served in a Styrofoam cup with a lid on it and a piece of tape over the opening for the straw. They also have to give you the straw wrapped in paper, not inserted in the cup. As long as you don't put the straw in it or remove the straw or lid, you are legal. I don't condone drinking and driving one bit, but I do like the fact that I can get an icy cold adult beverage at my favorite daiquiri shop.

✦ Hair of the Dog That Bit You Milk Punch

This New Orleans milk punch is in the tradition of the Bloody Mary and other hangover drink remedies. If you're enjoying it in the morning after a long night out, think about adding a shot or two of espresso for a whole different but still delicious drink. Watch out: It's so tasty, you'll want to be sure the cure doesn't become the cause! New Orleans milk punch also makes a delightful lighter alternative to classic eggnog, and if you want to get fancy, you can make milk ice cubes to serve in the milk punch.

Serves 4

2 cups brandy
1 cup dark crème de cacao
2 cups whole milk
freshly grated nutmeg

Chill 4 (10-ounce) Collins glasses in the freezer. In a 2-quart container with a lid, combine the brandy, crème de cacao, and milk. Shake until well mixed and place in the freezer until cold. Shake again and divide among the 4 cold glasses. Top with a grating of fresh nutmeg. You can also serve this over ice if you don't want to wait for it to get cold in the fridge.

✦ Victor's Brandy Alexander

Dubbed "the original chocolate martini," the Brandy Alexander is a sweet brandy-based cocktail that became popular during the early twentieth century. It has always been a popular New Orleans drink and was a favorite of playwright Tennessee Williams:

> "It was in New Orleans that I wrote most of A Streetcar Named Desire. At that time, I was under the mistaken impression that I was dying…When I had finished my work, I would go around the corner to a pleasant bar called Victor's and have myself a Brandy Alexander, which I thought would give me strength to get through the rest of the day. It was a somewhat irrational idea…but without that idea of imminent death I doubt I could have created Blanche DuBois."

Serves 1

1 ounce brandy
1 ounce dark crème de cacao
1 ounce heavy cream

crushed ice
pinch of freshly ground nutmeg, for
    garnish

Shake all the ingredients together in a cocktail shaker with ice and strain into martini glass. Garnish with nutmeg and serve.

City That Care Forgot Brulée

Although crème brûlée is not unique to New Orleans, it is a very popular dessert here and some of the best versions are served in the restaurants of the city. I came up with this drink on a cold, rainy day. The delicious blend of Grand Marnier, amaretto, crème de cacao, and cream is broiled as it would be for a crème brûlée. You certainly won't have any cares after sipping on one of these.

Serves 1

1 ounce Grand Marnier
¾ ounce amaretto
½ ounce white crème de cacao

lightly whipped cream, for topping
orange zest, for garnish
sugar, for topping

Chill a 3-ounce martini glass. Shake the Grand Marnier, amaretto, and white crème de cacao with ice in a cocktail shaker and strain into the chilled glass. Top with a layer of lightly whipped cream. Garnish with thin strips of orange zest and sugar. Use a kitchen torch to broil the sugar until it crystallizes and serve.

Rock You Like a (Purple) Hurricane

This one is the creation of my dear mixologist friend Helena Tiare Olsen, the biggest fan of the Tremé in Sweden. Thanks, girl! Warning: This smooth and yummy drink goes down real easy but is very alcoholic, and if you're not careful, you could find yourself standing on the levee in your birthday suit, singing "Walking to New Orleans"!

Serves 1

crushed ice
3 ounces Smith and Cross rum
1 ounce freshly squeezed lime juice
1 ounce freshly squeezed lemon
    juice
1 tablespoon passion fruit syrup
1 ounce simple syrup

1 tablespoon hibiscus grenadine
½ tablespoon blue curaçao
lime slice, for garnish
fresh mint, for garnish
black cherries, for garnish
Lemon Hart 151 proof (generous
    for a real kick)

Half-fill a tall Collins glass with crushed ice. Shake the rum, lime juice, lemon juice, passion fruit syrup, simple syrup, hibiscus grenadine, and blue curaçao in a cocktail shaker with no ice. Pour unstrained into the glass. Fill the glass with more ice and garnish with a lime slice, fresh mint, and black cherries. Float the 151 rum on top. You can ignite the rum for visual effects.

Bourbon Street

You mention New Orleans to most anyone and they will ask you about Bourbon Street. This strip running from Canal Street to Esplanade is one of the most visited tourist attractions in the world. It's home to many restaurants, bars (gay and straight), hotels, B&Bs, and shops, as well as some of the best-known strip clubs in the world. Many assume that Bourbon Street is named because of the tons of alcohol that is served and consumed there, but it was really named in the early 1700s by the engineer, Adrien de Pauger, who is credited with designing the layout of the city's streets. The street is actually named for France's ruling family at the time, the House of Bourbon.

Bourbon Street is a great place to visit with a few caveats: this is not really a place to take the kids. There's not a whole lot going on during the day, except during festivals like Mardi Gras and Southern Decadence, which has been described as the largest gay street fair in the world. This celebration of NOLA's gay community has grown to epic proportions since its inception in 1972, and now attracts 100,000 to 300,000 participants, including international members of the LGBT community. With an economic windfall for the city of $100 to $200 million annually, attempts by religious groups to end the event have been thwarted by the business community and local policy makers. So know that if you visit the Quarter on Labor Day weekend, you'll find the Vieux Carré to be very gay, in both senses of the word.

Year-round, the action on Bourbon Street occurs after the sun goes down and continues on all night until sunrise the next morning. Many locals avoid the area, preferring to frequent other establishments outside of the more touristy sections of the city.

✦ New Orleans Lady

This is another one from my good friend Helena Tiare Olsen. The combination of rum, raspberry liqueur, pink champagne, and rose petals gives it a sassy style that will drive you crazy!

1½ ounces white rum
1½ ounces crème de framboise
pink champagne or sparkling rosé
    wine
1 pink rose petal, for garnish

Chill a champagne coupe, champagne flute, or martini glass. Shake the rum and crème de framboise in a cocktail shaker with ice, and strain into the chilled glass. Top with pink champagne or sparkling rosé wine, and garnish with a pink rose petal.

Tipitina's

After Katrina, the non-profit Tipitina Foundation came to be an integral part of the resurrection of the music scene in the city, providing services and new instruments to displaced musicians who needed help getting their lives back together. The foundation has also become active in the promotion of music education in the city and provides seminars and workshops to the future musicians who call New Orleans home. To find out more and see how you can help, visit their website at tipitinasfoundation.org.

Appendix

Of pure magic you were born,
Like music from Satchmo's horn.
May your life be filled with jazz,
All the beauty this world has,
May joie de vivre fill your soul,
May good gumbo fill your bowl.
Only sweet things lie in store...
As New Orleans thrives once more.
May the monkeys ask for you,
Down at the Audubon Zoo.
May the storms in life be mild...

For you, the mighty Storm Child!

From Storm Child by Todd-Michael St. Pierre

Conversions

MEASURE	EQUIVALENT	METRIC
1 teaspoon	--	5.0 milliliters
1 tablespoon	3 teaspoons	14.8 milliliters
1 cup	16 tablespoons	236.8 milliliters
1 pint	2 cups	473.6 milliliters
1 quart	4 cups	947.2 milliliters
1 liter	4 cups + 3½ tablespoons	1000 milliliters
1 ounce (dry)	2 tablespoons	28.35 grams
1 pound	16 ounces	453.49 grams
2.21 pounds	35.3 ounces	1 kilogram
325°F/350°F/375°F	--	165°C/177°C/190°C

Photo Credits

p. 5 © Daniel Sieradski

p. 7 © Vamsi K. H. Illindala

p. 10 © Diane Millsap/www.neworleans-art.net

p. 13 © David Vance

p. 15 © Terry Poche/shutterstock.com

p. 16 © Ron Weinstock

p. 21 top © Kevin & Debbie Rudd; bottom © Michael Zaffuto

p. 22 © Diane Millsap/www.neworleans-art.net

p. 25 © Christine King

p. 29 © Jennifer Yost

p. 33 © judiswinksphotography.com

p. 36 © Randall Kooistra

p. 40 © Anthony Turducken Del Rosario

p. 44 © judiswinksphotography.com

p. 48 © Diane Millsap/www.neworleans-art.net

p. 50 © Daniel Sieradski

p. 53 © judiswinksphotography.com

p. 54 top © Leigh Hennessy Robson; bottom © Daniel Sieradski

p. 62 top © RV Schexnayder; bottom © Daniel Sieradski

p. 64 © Stacey M. Warnke

p. 67 © judiswinksphotography.com

p. 72 © Jon Belanger

p. 77 top © Milan Ilnyckyj/sindark.com; bottom © jimscottphotos.com

p. 78 © judiswinksphotography.com

p. 84 © judiswinksphotography.com

p. 89 © Sarah Hales

p. 91 © judiswinksphotography.com

p. 92 © jimscottphotos.com

p. 102 © judiswinksphotography.com

p. 105 © Caleb White

p. 107 © Patrick Lamont/shutterstock.com

p. 111 © RV Schexnayder

p. 112 © Diane Millsap/www.neworleans-art.net

p. 119 © judiswinksphotography.com

p. 125 © Ray Gould

p. 128 © judiswinksphotography.com

Recipe Index